Advance Pr~~~ ~~~

DAY BY DAY

"When serious illness strikes a child, the blow hits all family members with horrifying ferocity. Often, while the adults are reeling from that devastating impact, the purity of the feelings and spirit of a young sibling can provide strength which sustains all."

— RICHARD EDELSON, MD, director, Yale Cancer Center

"Siblings many times are the "silent warriors" in the childhood cancer fight. They deeply feel the joys and pains associated with their family's journey. Within *Day By Day,* there are stories from the sibling perspective that demonstrate the great depth of their experience."

— TRACY MOORE, LCSW, Director of Support Services, Children's Brain Tumor Foundation

"I think that *Day By Day* will help families, and siblings who read it understand that they are not alone in their experiences. It can often be isolating and overwhelming for children and parents when there is a child or sibling who is chronically ill in the family. The stories and perspectives shared in the book are empowering and hopefully will help facilitate positive coping."

— ERIN SPAULDING, MS, CCLS, Child Life Specialist, Yale-New Haven Hospital

"Siblings of sick children need the support of teachers more than ever because the parents are overwhelmed and stressed by the caring of the child that is sick. Parents can only do so much in one day. If the sibling has someone in their daily life that can take on the role of a caretaker that is concerned and willing to listen, it helps the sibling gain confidence that they are in good hands. I think reading a book about someone's personal experience, as in *Day By Day*, gives people in similar situations great comfort and guidance. The sibling is hurting inside because they want to make everything better when they have no control over the situation. They want their sibling to be well and they want their parents back to 'normal'. Kids crave to be normal."

—CLAIRE VIOLA EGAN, MS Education

DAY BY DAY

CHRISTINE FRISBEE

DAY
BY DAY

Children tell their journeys of

faith and determination

living with a sick sister or brother

FRISBEE FOUNDATION PUBLISHING

New York

Dedication

TO MY SON, RICH, who showed us the meaning of life and who asked that I "not let this happen to others." Thank you for the blessings you brought into my life. My love for you is as strong as the day you came into our lives and the day you left us.

To my other four children, Kirsten, Jim, Meg and Mary Jane. You taught me through your strength, love and laughter. To my husband, Rick. I thank you for your patience and guidance to pursue this dream. This book would never have come to be if we all did not take Rich's journey in life with his effervescent personality and his fight to get well.

To my extraordinary parents, Mary Jane and Jim Kenny and my eleven sisters and brothers. You taught me how special it is to be part of such a warm family. This added untold depth to this work.

Contents

DAY BY DAY

Introduction

WHO WOULD THINK that if you have a sibling who is always sick, you could be happy and offer hope and inspiration to others? Yet we found this to be very true by listening to the sisters and brothers in these families!

Children who have a sister or brother with a chronic illness, severe handicap or mental disability can offer some of the best advice to live by, each day of our lives. We discovered this in a very personal way and realized we must pass this message on to others.

This book is for families but also for doctors, medical students, nurses, teachers, social workers and all caretakers. It is for each and every one of us who care enough to allow the siblings to have a voice and in order to bring understanding about their challenges.

While independent studies have been written on the repercussions of families coping with a sick child, it has not been addressed in book form with voices by the children until now. Sadly, I think this is indicative of the problem itself—these are forgotten children. The importance of their feelings has been diminished by the enormity of the issues for the sick child himself. They feel as though "the world is falling out from under them."

It may seem unfathomable, but there is nothing in medical school curriculum that instructs the future doctors of the world on the effect a child's illness has on their sisters and brothers. Doctors and caregivers are not taught how to deal with the challenges and the vulnerability of these siblings as they struggle and live with extraordinary fear and pain, and simultaneously deal with the normal challenges of growing up and being a regular kid.

It is estimated that between fourteen and sixteen million families live with a child who has a chronic illness, yet there is little available to help with the many emotional issues that surround these families. The brothers and sisters of the sick children watch from the sidelines with little assistance from the world. Yet they live lives emotionally way beyond the expectations of normal childhood existence. How do these siblings go through life with less time and attention from their parents? What do they do with their anger? Who is to understand their isolation? How can they answer the questions that pound in their heads: Why did this happen? Why me? Am I selfish? Why do I wish it were me instead?

The long term affects of chronic illness on children and their siblings shows that these children are at a greater risk for psychological problems including emotional disorders, abnormal behavior and school adjustment problems. Despite these sobering statistics, there is evidence that in some families, there are positive long term benefits to growing up with an ill sibling. The sisters and brothers show greater compassion for others. This finding is supported by the recurring themes you will read in the stories presented in our book.

Our observations and research showed that the severity or complexity of the illness is not always as significant on the family dynamics as the emotions that result from the illness. Once the diagnosis is made, each family forms their own patterns and family dynamics that differentiate them from other families. We aim to heighten the awareness of the impact of illness within families that results in a different style of child rearing separating them from the lives of their peers.

This difference in the family's imposed lifestyle can result in sibling emotions of anger, isolation, fear and guilt as they wrestle with their feelings and grasp for their own time and attention from the parents. This is all being attempted without enough assistance and guidance from adults.

Some of the stories tell of children who did not survive and while this is the reality with some childhood illnesses many more live with chronic illnesses. In reaching out to families for stories we had contacts with social workers that helped families with childhood cancer therefore several of the stories come from siblings of children with leukemia. It is important to mention that childhood leukemia is one of the most curable childhood cancers today. The stories here are not a true representation of the statistics for leukemia but are the stories from my children and others that we knew who contributed to *Day By Day*.

Our mission is to guide families away from shock and fear, towards acceptance and healing. Poignant lessons will be taught through the stories written by these sisters and brothers. The stories display many focused emotions that help bring to light the raw feelings that these families live with. The stories are grouped into chapters that introduce the reader to various stages and sentiments that affect not only the child but the entire family.

The beginnings of the children's stories are sometimes stark in their portrayal of the shock and denial that is their experience. With time and acceptance they do eventually evolve into positive growth. Therefore, the stories are staged in what might be called a typical progression of emotions.

Moving from the initial shock and negative emotions, the book naturally evolves as the children's stories themselves draw the reader to reflect on the peace and acceptance each family reaches in its own personal way.

The highlight of the final few chapters poignantly demonstrates how the family inexplicably embraces the situation and how their determination and faith light the way.

The children are not sorry that the illness entered into their family, but in fact say that in retrospect and with time, they experienced positive benefits hidden within their difficult situation. Through these personal stories, the voices of the siblings reflect insight, faith and peace as they mature beyond their years.

Chapter 1

A SIGNIFICANT MOMENT

*"I realized how the journey to help
Rich get through his illness changed us all forever."*

*"Parenting classes don't prepare us to raise
a child with a disability or illness, and when it
happens none of the rulebooks apply."*

I LIVED EVERY mother's nightmare, and my husband and our four other children went to hell and back with me. Everything that happened during that time, and since, has changed who we are and how we look at life forever. Today we are stronger, more serene and more peaceful than we've ever been—even more than before tragedy struck. The experience left me with a passion to pass onto others what my family has learned: how we were torn apart and came together again, and how our children were part of the healing process.

We feel blessed to have a wonderful family and address each day with joy and faith. We have adjusted to our life's challenges and are able to move forward. It is a journey that continues to take a lot of work, but it also brings us peace to be able to reach out to others and support them as well.

It only took 24 hours to change my life forever. My journey began one day in September of 1988 when our son Rich came home from school in tears of exhaustion complaining that he was tired and could not run down the soccer field. Rich, a healthy, athletic 14 year old, had an occasional taste

for getting into a bit of trouble. He was an incredible run-
ner, good student and had very nice friends. As his mother,
I concluded that his new high school schedule might be too
strenuous; one day home would enable him to catch up on
the sleep he needed. The next day he lay on the sofa with
aching pains feeling faint and I knew that he needed to see
Dr. Flynn, our pediatrician. The visit was not your typical
visit. He was poked and prodded, had blood tests and chest
x-rays and then we were sent home with instructions to call
the doctor that evening.

Dr. Flynn's message that night was calm but very specific,
"Rich has something serious, a blood disease; you need to go
to Yale-New Haven Hospital in the morning. You have an
8:30 appointment. Go to the emergency room. Dr. Diana
Beardsley will be expecting you."

The emergency room glass doors shut firmly behind us
as we cautiously walked towards the desk to fill out forms.
Worrying about what was ahead of us, I thought it must be a
mistake, or maybe a dream and I tried to wake myself from
the nightmare, but within an hour we were told Rich had leukemia. So our journey began and our lives quickly unraveled.
I felt like I had been pushed out of an airplane with a parachute. As I fell towards the ground my heart pounded and I
couldn't breath. I was scared I would not be able to open the
parachute. I reached back but couldn't find the cord. A voice
called to me, "Pull the cord, its' behind you, pull it!" and I fell
to the ground, bruised and exhausted from the fall.

How quickly things change. One day Rich was fine, and
the next day our lives were in shambles. No one in the family
even knew what leukemia was and no one could tell us what
the future held. It was impossible for anyone to grasp the
intensity of my husband's and my fear and confusion: not the
doctors, not my parents, not any of our four other children. It

was something we never dreamed would happen to us.

Friday I was driving the children to school, and Saturday I was standing in a hospital linen room surrounded by white folded bed sheets, tied in bundles, doubled over in pain. Tears came down my face as I angrily told Dr. Flynn, "This was not supposed to happen to me, this only happens to other people." He offered a promise that I couldn't believe at the time, "You will make it through." The doctors and nurses were kind and honest—no one told us it wouldn't be hard or made any empty promises.

Parenting classes don't prepare us to raise a child with a disability or illness, and when it happens none of the rule-books apply. I had no idea how my mothering skills would transfer from making three healthy meals a day to chasing between home and the hospital for a year. I will always remember how numb with fear I was those days. Each morning I dutifully dressed and fed my four other children and then rushed to tend to Rich at the hospital. Kirsten, Jim, Meg and Mary Jane were scared and scattered. I didn't think our family would get through the pain and emotional torture.

At the beginning of my journey, I felt like a skydiver taking a new dive each and every day. I scrambled to find my parachute chord and was scared to fall. Everyday I hit the ground hard, covered with bruises. But I finally learned how to open the parachute so that I glided and landed safely. Although it took some time, I was braver but wiser. Everyday I would pray to God to give me the strength to deal with what was ahead of me.

Fifteen months later Rich had undergone intense chemotherapy, a bone marrow transplant and then relapsed with leukemia. He lost his effort to go on. He knew he was losing the battle with his disease. We all told him we loved him. He told us he would be with us, just from a different place. I feel him with me every day.

In one of Rich's last conversations with me he said "Mom, make sure this doesn't happen to somebody else." That was a significant moment in my life. I realized how the journey to help Rich get through his illness changed us all forever.

My new mission on life was to make a difference in the lives of other families who were going through what we had gone through. We were encouraged by friends to start a foundation and raise money to help others. In 1990 we had established the Richard D. Frisbee III Foundation. Our mission is to support basic and clinical research to further understanding and treatment for childhood and adult cancers and related bone marrow diseases; advance the application of bone marrow and stem cell transplantation for treatment; establish support systems for patients and their families during treatment and provide ongoing educational programs for health care professionals. The Foundation grew over the years and we have funded programs that reach beyond our initial mission. We have awarded research grants at eight universities, supported over 20 nursing scholarships, provided housing for patients who travel distances for medical care, encouraged support groups for siblings and art therapy for families and funded one of the most sophisticated research labs in the country at Yale-New Haven Hospital that has enabled over 1000 patients live longer lives.

I returned to school to study social work at Columbia University, but before finishing, I was recruited to apply for a position at the Yale School of Medicine as Coordinator for the Unrelated Donor Program. It was a wonderful job where I would help find donors for families who needed a donor for a bone marrow transplant. We would type the family member's blood for antigens that identified the immune system. It took weeks to get results and I would council the families while we searched the bone marrow registries. Eventually I took on the role as the Administrator for the Bone Marrow and Stem Cell Transplant Program.

Through this experience, I came to learn so much more about what the families were feeling and I absorbed so much strength and love from this special group of families. One of the most significant things I came to understand is that there is a common thread holding together all of the families who have a sick child: a thread of trust and faith that they will make it through their struggle and lead happy lives. This thread also connects the sisters and brothers because they all share the fears, disappointments, hopes and dreams.

The mothers, fathers and children that visited the clinic came from every socio-economic background, with various levels of education and different levels of understanding of their diagnosis. While sitting with them and talking, it was clear to me that the diagnosis of the child affected the entire family. Day after day and week after week, they sat together in the clinic and each family connected to the other as they waited and hoped that things would get better. Some families had good news but others faced constant disappointment and all the while the siblings sat and watched, processing the situation on their own while the parents concentrated their energy on the sick child. As these siblings sat watching for minutes or hours, their perspective on life gradually changed.

My relationships with the children made me appreciate the patience of my own children while we were hoping that Rich would make it in his battle. The book was initiated when I asked my own children to write about what it was like for them to have a sick brother. You will see their stories in this book. They each tell their own story; each one is different.

Having been raised in a very large family with twelve children, I am keenly aware of the impact of sibling relationships. I pick up every book and article I see to better understand the complex dynamics that these relationships form over a life-time. As every child perceives their value in the family as they grow up, imagine the significance of this when there is a sick child in the family. The reassessing that occurs within these children is dramatic and life-changing. The level of commu-nication, the strength of the family structure and often their faith in God influence the sibling's ability to cope.

We cannot underestimate the impact that an illness has on the sisters and brothers of the sick child. Cindy Crawford, model, actress and mother, wrote in Marlo Thomas's Book *The Right Words at the Right Time* about her brother's illness with leukemia and ultimate death. "It was the most significant thing that affected my life."

In the July 10, 2006 issue of *Time* magazine, Wendy Cole, in her article "The New Science of Siblings," writes about the great importance of brothers and sisters. She notes that in a research study done at Penn State University in 1996, they discovered that the amount of time spent between siblings in any day is greater than the time spent with parents, friends or teachers. They estimate that this time makes up 33% of a child's day. She says, "It's your brothers and sisters who shape you." With the great influence that sibling relationships play in how a child perceives themselves, take into account that 5% of the children in America have a sister or brother who is chronically ill or mentally challenged.

My journey in writing this book brought me in touch with amazing professionals. I had many discussions with nurses and doctors, social workers and teachers over the importance of this subject. One summer break from college, our daugh-ter, Mary Jane, helped to work on the book as an assistant and intern. During that time, she contacted   Connie Nicolosi, Pediatric Oncology Social Worker and Erin Spaulding, Child Life Specialist, at Yale-New Haven Hospital. These dynamic and caring professionals run support groups for siblings of children with any illness. They have developed group sessions where children can discuss their stories and express the emotions that they feel in a completely safe atmosphere. Saturday workshops are held where these children come together to share their stories and feelings as they comfort each other through their expressions of fear and hope under the guidance of these professionals. They have been invaluable in helping to gather stories for this book and provided a forum for Mary Jane to give a presentation to the families who have someone who is or was undergoing treatment at Yale-New Haven Hospital. We are very grateful for all of the stories we received from this group of families.

Richard Edelson, MD, director of Yale Cancer Center asked if he could read some of the stories that we had at the time. He wrote back to me saying how much of an impact these stories of love had on him. He said that although he had taken care of patients for many years, he did not fully grasp the influence of illness on the siblings. He said that one of the missing components of medical school is that there is nothing taught to young medical students about the significance of looking at the entire family when treating a patient.

Diana Beardsley, MD, PhD, Pediatric Hematologist and Oncologist and Professor at the Yale School of Medicine recently invited me to be part of a panel to educate second year medical students at Yale in the importance of communication with families during diagnosis, treatment and ongoing care. The person interviewing me, Laurie Cardona, Psy. D. Chief of Psychology at the Yale Child Study Center, has much experience in working with families who live with a sick child. Her sensitive and gentle interview enabled me to tell stories that are hard to re-live and often still bring tears to my eyes, as they did that day.

I am pleased to say the students' response was amazing. They were keenly interested in the dynamics of a family with a sick child. Many of them wiped their tears as they realized the potential power of what they might offer families with kind words and understanding. They asked wonderful questions about the other children in the family, how they responded, what their fears were and how I tried to help them. One of the stories she asked me about was the day we brought Rich to the hospital and heard his diagnosis from the doctors. I now call that day "the first day of the rest of my life."

Anita Nirenberg, MS, RN, Assistant Professor of Clinical Nursing, Columbia University School of Nursing, has done important research on family dynamics when a child is seriously ill. Her interest in the subject brought us together to discuss the topic of siblings and their significant role in the family as well as their unspoken needs. Her immense appreciation of the challenges of these families has brought her to devoting time on the board of the Brain Tumor Foundation. She has watched many families struggle through the shock of diagnosis through the challenges of day to day living to acceptance and healing.

The Leukemia and Lymphoma Society was one of the first patient support organizations that established a program for teachers in schools where there are children with cancer and other blood related diseases. The program was developed to bring a better understanding not only of what the sick child endures but also the consequences and impact of their treatment when the students return to school and the impact on the other members of the family.

Claire Viola Egan, one of our children's grammar school teachers, was one of the first teachers to go through the program. Her mother's battle with leukemia when she was a child brought insight into what our family was going though. I asked Claire what she would say to readers of this book. She replied,

"Siblings of sick children need the support of teachers more than ever because the parents are overwhelmed and stressed by the caring of the child that is sick. Parents can only do so much in one day. If the sibling has someone in their daily life that can take on the role of a caretaker that is concerned and willing to listen, it helps the sibling gain confidence that they are in good hands. I think reading a book about someone's personal experience like yours would give people in similar situations great comfort and guidance. The sibling is hurting inside because they want to make everything better when they have no control over the situation. They want their sibling to be well and they want their parents back to 'normal'. Kids crave to be normal."

Judy Solomon, MSW and Erin Goldring, MA Child-life Specialist at the Hackensack Children's Hospital in New Jersey, worked closely with us to get stories for our book They are also affiliated with Tomorrows Children, an organization started by radio personality Don Imus and his wife, Dierdre. Enthusiastic and very helpful, they were so knowledgeable about the need for this book and were eager to gather stories which added a huge amount of both knowledge and content. As professionals, they recognized the difficulty in getting the stories, knowing that not all siblings want to discuss their feelings or even more so, to write their emotions down.

We see our book as the first in a series of stepping-stones that will teach siblings how to ride the waves of uncertainty and feel in control of their emotions.

My prayer is that we help many families in their journey to find Hope.

Chapter 2

FIRST CONFUSION, THEN DENIAL

"When I first learned that he was sick, I was completely lost." —JAMES

"I wish my mother had told me more, but I did figure it out." —ROBERT

THIS CHAPTER IDENTIFIES the truthful feelings of a sibling who has recently discovered that a brother or sister has an illness or disability. The stories demonstrate the shock of diagnosis. This is the initial stage when the child says to himself, How could this happen? Why is it happening? It shouldn't happen. I don't want it to be true. It is the reaction of shock and disbelief that is a wave of new feelings where they do not know how to identify the complexity of their natural reaction. Frequently it is beyond their childlike comprehension.

Children need adults to help them cope with the initial diagnosis and the onslaught of feelings that bring with them chaos and uncertainty. They are faced with a myriad of internal and external pressures. Often parents are overwhelmed by their own emotions and may not be able to be a comfort to the other children.

While once their lives were just like their friends, now they are forever different. Siblings are frightened and con-

fused when they do not understand the reality of the diagnosis and often their first instinct is to deny the reality as a way
of coping with all of the shock and uncertainty. The family
is diffused with new pressures on all family members. There
are demands on the children to contribute to family chores,
while the parents now have increased financial pressure and
challenging time allotments. And all this is demanded while
they work through the initial shock of the diagnosis.

Parents are forced into a new world of complex medical information. They listen while they hedge the long term
prognosis. Interpreting the complicated treatment is usually
extremely difficult for parents themselves, and they then try
to explain to the other children in the family what is happening to their sister or brother. They may not even know. One
way to assist children with the enormous changes happening
in their surroundings is to discuss the changes that are occur-
ring in the family in an age appropriate way. Once discussed,
children will grow with the information if the delivery is con-
sistent and it is spoken with concern and support.

In *The Empty Room,* Elizabeth DeVita Rathburn tells her
rendering of her brother's diagnosis with the intense sensi-
tivity of a child. As a result of her brother's illness Elizabeth
spent most of her childhood going to the hospital to visit her
brother. She poignantly describes how one day she and her
brother, Ted, were playing in the yard and the next day he
was in the hospital. While Elizabeth did not understand what
was happening, her father, an oncologist, was unfortunately
too aware of the path of their journey. Suddenly her brother
and her hero were living in the hospital in a protective bubble
because of his failing immune system. She could not touch
her brother because of his illness and their father could not
cure him. They were all devastated.

Like Elizabeth's story, the children in this chapter identify the honest feelings of siblings who have recently discovered a brother or sister's illness. Some demonstrate the child's shock of diagnosis, yet almost all end with resolution and words of faith and strength.

As you read and listen to the children's stories themselves, with their honesty and directness, you learn about what it was like for them to enter into the world of becoming the "other child". These children are hopeful, direct and in many ways wiser than adults. Through their ability to write these stories, the children exemplify angels that are trying to tell us what we need to hear and know to assist them.

JAMES, 27, SAN DIEGO
My Fallen Hero

Although it's been almost seventeen years since my brother passed away, I can still remember the details of this life-changing experience. It all seemed to happen so fast. In only two years, my life had taken on a whole new reality, and I was only 10 years old.

When I first learned that Rich was sick, I was completely lost. My parents did their best to explain, but I couldn't comprehend what had happened. I didn't understand what leukemia was, or what bone marrow was, or why my brother wasn't coming home that afternoon. The only thing that I understood was that he was going to be in the hospital for a long time. What did this mean to me? That Rich was going to be the center of attention . . . as usual. I was jealous. Rich had always been in the limelight, and now he was getting even more attention. It wasn't fair. Of course, at this age, I didn't fully understand that leukemia is a life-threatening disease, so I thought everything was eventually going to be fine and soon enough he would be back to being my typical older brother.

That feeling of jealousy was gone the first time I saw my big brother laying in a hospital bed. I remember seeing my parents and my older sister in tears about all of this, but I still didn't understand why. I remember thinking, "Rich was going to be fine. Why is everyone so upset?" Then, as we entered his hospital room, and I saw my brother lying in a metal frame bed and hooked up to machines, I almost tried to convince myself I was lost in a dream. What was going on? This can't be my brother. It was only then that I understood the magnitude of the situation and why everyone was being so emotional. I had never seen my brother so fragile.

Only two days before, he had me pinned to the ground giving me a Charlie-horse because I borrowed his Walkman without asking, and now this? That two-day period he was in the hospital changed how I envisioned my brother. He had been poked and prodded, hooked up to machines, and now looked more fragile than ever. Someone who I had looked up to my whole life was now looking at me with fear in his eyes. I had never seen that before, and it scared me.

Over then next six months or so, I became an expert on leukemia. It's all that was ever discussed. What was Rich's platelet count? Is his food staying down? How is he reacting to the chemotherapy? It was a barrage of information that I soaked up like a sponge. At the age of 10 I had become an educator in my own school. My friends would ask how my brother was doing and I would respond with some hospital jargon that none of them would understand, but it made me feel important. I was doing my brother justice by spreading the knowledge.

It was a difficult time for me. My grades were slipping, my parents never seemed to be around, so it was hard to be able hang out with my friends on the weekend, and I had taken on some hefty new responsibilities. My two younger sisters needed someone to help with their schoolwork, or make dinner, or answer their questions about Rich. That was me, and I was glad to do it.

When we would get to go to the hospital to see Rich, usually on the weekends, we would spend that time playing Nintendo with him, or walking around the hospital with him. Rich was usually in a wheelchair or on crutches due to his weakened state, but he would never let me see that he was unable to do anything. He was my older brother and was "supposed" to be stronger than me, and he always made sure of that. I never wanted to talk about how he was feeling, or what his medication was doing, I just wanted to make sure he was still having fun. He was only 14 when diagnosed, and deserved to still live the life a 14-year-old would. I felt helpless, though. We couldn't go ride our bikes, or go to the movies, or play basketball. So I did what I could. I only hope that he enjoyed what time we had together.

After a bone marrow transplant, donated by my younger sister Meg, Rich went into a brief remission. We all felt as though the leukemia had been overcome, but the most devastating news came during our summer vacation in Cape Cod when we learned that Rich had relapsed, and not only that, but the leukemia was stronger and growing faster than before. Our summer vacation was cut short, and again, Rich went back into the hospital.

Unfortunately, this time around, the chemotherapy was not working and his only slim chance at recovery would be another bone marrow transplant. Visiting the hospital after Rich had relapsed was unbearable. He looked more unhealthy than I had ever seen him. So thin, weak, and almost unable to speak. It was as though I could see the leukemia eating away

at him in front of my eyes. It was unbearable and very difficult to watch. The chances of Rich actually surviving another
bone marrow transplant surgery were slim. He wasn't strong
enough and chose not to go through it again. I hated him for
this. How could he give up? Why would he? He had been so
strong this whole time, and now it was over? He had never
given up on anything in his life! Again . . . I was confused.

It was only a matter of time before the end. I wish that I
was with him when he passed on. Maybe my parents didn't
want me to be there because it would have been too hard,
maybe there wasn't enough time, or maybe he asked for his
siblings not to be there, I don't know. I felt and still do feel
as though I deserved to be next to him. He was and still is the
only person that I consider my hero.

Now that I've grown and am able reflect on the experience,
I wish there were many things that I had told my brother before he passed away. Many things that I wish we were able to
do together. My brother's experience is a perfect example of
how something like this can happen instantaneously, and no
one can be prepared. Because of it, I've learned that I need to
live every day as though it could be my last. Rich will always
remain in my heart and I know that he is with me in spirit. I
look forward to the day we meet again.

ROBERT, NEW YORK

I was six when my brother was born with an enlarged kidney.
I tried to understand how sick my baby brother was. Everyone was busy trying to figure out how to keep him alive but
no one told me that my brother was also mentally retarded
and that our life would never be the same. The hospital visits
and the diagnoses of mental retardation left my mother de-

pressed. I wish my mother had told me more, but I did figure it out. I have taken care of my brother my whole life, even now, and he is still getting into trouble. But he is my brother and I love him.

WENDRYN, 30, SPARKS, NEVADA

When I was taking classes at Mills College, I had something of an epiphany regarding Daniel. I was taking a class called "The Sociology of Death and Dying." It was fascinating and it was also hard work emotionally. The instructor required us to think about all of the aspects of death, dying, and how our society reacts to death and deals with it (or does its best to avoid dealing with it). Anyway, one of the speakers had a younger sister with a disability and was talking about going through the stages of grief as he learned to accept her. He went through the same stages of grief, including anger and denial, which people go through while dealing with death.

I felt like the breath had been knocked out of me. I had spent my life so far trying, I suppose, to be a champion for Daniel. His room was right next to mine, so when he had night terrors when he was little I was the one who got up with him, and it actually got to the point that I would wake up a couple of minutes before he did because I hated being woken up by his yells. I had tried so hard to get people to accept him and look at him that I hadn't stepped back and allowed myself the grief that does come with living with someone with a disability.

In my family, younger siblings were supposed to be taken care of by the older ones. Family was the most important thing in life, and we were responsible for each other. Because I was second in the birth order, my younger sister and younger brother were both, to me, my responsibility to some extent. This was much more true with Daniel than with Margaret because Daniel was much younger than I. I hadn't ever allowed myself to be angry at Daniel for being different. I was supposed to take care of him, I was responsible for him, and it wasn't his fault that he was different, so I had no right to be angry with him.

My mom was great. She told me she thought we knew it was okay. She let me vent, let me cry, and helped me work through it. I had felt such a sense of responsibility and of the unfairness of it all that, without even registering that there was anger involved, I had shoved it down as far as I possibly could so I didn't have to pay attention to it. I couldn't accept being angry at Daniel, especially when he was little and helpless. I couldn't deal with it as he got older, either, because he was working so hard just to make life work for him that for me to get angry at him would have been adding insult to injury.

I have been through all of the stages of grief about Down syndrome now. I have worked my way to a point of acceptance, of knowing that much of who Daniel is and what I love about him results from his disability. I understand that each of us in his family and everyone he has come into contact with has been changed by him, even if it is only in a small way.

I still have work to do. I am still sometimes embarrassed when people clearly feel awkward around Daniel, and I have a fierce protectiveness towards him. The protectiveness is not bad, I think, but I am glad to be living somewhere else so I do not interfere in his life. He does have a life that works, and he is a good person. He is learning to fit into the world he lives in. It's hard for me to hear people talking about Daniel as if he can't hear them and to see his face change. I know he understands. I know it hurts him. I know that, short of confronting people (which would embarrass him more if I did it right then and there), I can't do anything about it. People will learn to accept him or not, but it can't be my fight all of the time.

MARK, 10, GREENWICH, CONNECTICUT

I found out my brother had cancer on the school bus. It was in second grade. My parents did not want me to know how sick Todd was. They told me that Todd had a disease that made him weak. But then my friend told me he had the big "C". That meant cancer. I did not think my friend was right. It turns out my parents told my friend's parents but not me. I was old enough to know. He was my little brother. I should know so that I could help him. That made me mad. Todd was my brother. I miss Todd.

———————

There is an underestimation in society as to how much we learn from children. We can see without distortion through the innocent and honest eyes of children and it is through listening to these children that we learn to reach an understanding and resolution. Once we hear what they say we must try to respond so that each child has an opportunity to grow in a healthy way. Through the children's strength we often find our own strength. We must not shy away from discussion or stay removed from the reality of what is happening.

The stories reveal the feelings of separation and anxiety because one is getting treatment for the illness while the other child tries to go on with their life. When there is an illness with imminent death, the children sometimes state that they want to be their when their sibling dies. The sick child may be far from the hospital and it may be impossible for the children to be together. This can have long term affects on the one left at home.

The best way to guide children through their confusion and isolation is to acknowledge their feelings and help them to discuss what they are thinking and how they view what is happening every day. Talking though their thoughts and worries will help them in their journey to acceptance and peace. Let the child open up and talk when you are able.

The children can begin to express their feelings through writing and drawing. This is very cathartic and therapeutic during stressful situations. While putting on paper the expression of emotions the reality is validated and becomes real and tangible. This is a significant step in healing. The level of artistic ability does not matter, but it is the expression that is the most important thing. Allow the children to express their confusion.

Chapter 3

ANGER

&

*"I never told my parents how I felt and did not
know anyone else who would understand."* —DANIELLE

*"As the sibling of a disabled person,
I felt like the unloved one at times."* —LINDSEY

THIS CHAPTER HELPS siblings to find ways to identify what their anger is trying to tell them. The feelings of frustration and anger emerge when a child realizes that their life is changing because of the sibling's situation. There is the acknowledgment that their lives are no longer normal. Happiness often disappears into a sense of distrust in the goodness of life. Anger is an appropriate way to feel when your life changes dramatically, and it's not always a bad thing.

"It's not anger itself that's a problem—it's how you handle it."

This is the belief of Robert T. Zackery, a licensed independent clinical social worker at the Mayo Clinic in Rochester, Minnesota. Zackery counsels people in how to manage their anger. Anger can lead to problem solving and the ability to take charge of a situation. Children often need guidance to help with anger because so many emotions can be felt when a sister or brother is sick or disabled. We all strive to have a normal, happy life. When the normal path changes, children are often angry and they may feel guilty about this anger, judging it as bad. They can feel trapped by what is happening and how it is dramatically changing their life. There is a chance that persistent depression can take hold when siblings feel life is out of control. Sometimes children feel they were the cause of their sibling's illness because of a recent argument or fight they had. They may think they "wished" something bad to happen to their sister or brother. This is quite common. Siblings can feel targeted as being bad or having been punished by an angry God who has singled them out. Through adult guidance this anger can be dissipated and alleviated. Often families who have a spiritual faith deal with anger through prayer, and acceptance of the different path their lives are taking. With adults surrounding them, offering constructive support, children can turn their fear and anger into the hope that things will get better. We found that when children were able to identify their anger they began to share their thoughts about how to see their new surroundings. Talking about feelings leads to a healing process. Once they heal they see the positive things that still do happen every day, despite the challenges they are faced with.

This understanding can be one of the most defining moments in their lives. When they speak or write about the new found feelings it allows the flow of their emotions to go from anger to hopeful and productive thoughts. Just as we think of physical exercise as relieving stress, children need outlets to express all of their issues during these times of change. Parents can assist children in defining their anger with specific exercises. These things can be accomplished in many ways through the expressions in art, creative writing and storytelling. Teachers can encourage students to tell their story to the class and encourage the love and support that can come with any wonderful story, in a secure setting.

Children need to have a "voice" about what is happening to them. Support groups, art therapy and just a good hug can be the answer to relieving the anger and frustration of children. By opening the door to their feelings and allowing outlets to express themselves, children will gain control of their anger and be able to move forward towards more positive expression of their feelings. There are exercises that may nudge the frustrating anger to allow better communication. We think that "mirror talking" is one wonderful way to allow children to express themselves. This is an exercise where siblings can talk in the mirror to themselves saying to their own person what they feel. They can learn to use the "voice" in the mirror to assert themselves intelligently and effectively. This will give them the confidence to say those same words to parents, teachers and caretakers. Think of it like practicing a script for a play. Seeing yourself in a mirror helps you visualize how you would verbalize your thoughts when you are ready.

For years studies have shown that families who have a strong faith often go through these times with more courage. Their faith enables them to talk about the fear and anger within the context of their beliefs. A priest, minister or rabbi can become another support system and reinforcement in these challenging times. Gradually there is a peace that occurs once the anger is spoken about and worked through as a family.

ARIEL, 16, NEW JERSEY

In my first memory, I am standing in the corner of my parents' darkened bedroom, lit only by a desk lamp on their night stand. I am facing their bed, where my mother and twin brother, David, are sitting. She is changing his broviac tube, or the tube that connects his IV to his bloodstream through a hole in his chest. In my memory, there is no sound or movement. It is just a single image of David, our mother and me in this darkened room, in a situation that still feels perfectly normal to me, but would likely remind most teenagers of a horror movie. David and I cannot be more than three years old.

Today, at age sixteen, we are both healthy. David has been in remission for the last ten years. This is not a fact I overlook, as it was not the definite outcome of his disease. However, his good health does not mean that all the aftereffects of his cancer are gone. I still feel, at times, less worthy, less noticed, less liked than he. The fact that David is charismatic, hilarious, and beautiful does not help this when *I* feel awkward and nervous in new social situations. I do not know for certain if this relates back to the way I grew up during four years of my early childhood, but I can't help but wonder if things would have been different if I had been the sick one, or if neither of us had cancer at all. But even reading that last sentence feels strange to me. David's sickness was part of my life and always will be. I know that I feel and think differently about cancer and other diseases than most people. I have been deeply, personally affected by a life-threatening illness, and I do not take lightly the impression that it left. I still know doctors and nurses at Hackensack Hospital where he was treated. We went to Disneyland when I was six as part of the Make-a-Wish Foundation, and we got to cut all the lines. Last year I read at my school's annual Relay for Life. When I see commercials for donations to cancer research facilities, I can't just be a little glum for the sixty seconds of my life they engage. I personally feel for each child whose sickly and frail image appears on the screen, knowing that they could have been my brother.

But how do these feelings correspond with the feelings of inadequacy, and, I'll admit, jealousy, I occasionally experience? Do I wish it had been me? Honestly, if I knew I would have survived like David did, yes. I wish I got the attention he got, and still gets today. I wish it was me who possesses that spark of life in David no one else seems able to touch. And why shouldn't he have developed such a spark, when he grew up with everyone rooting for him, everyone with their hopes pinned on his personal health and growth? I couldn't compete with that then, and I still can't today. Sometimes I wish I would get the debilitating illness, the paralyzing accident, so that my life could become the story of a shining child conquering the Great and Terrible Cancer. And I know this is a selfish, ungrateful, horrible thing to want. But I also know I'm not the only one who feels this way. Every person who has contributed to this book, and every sibling who reads it, has felt at least a tinge, if not more, of what I occasionally feel as well. And if one of you feels what I sometimes feel, then neither of us is the only one. We were all brought together in these pages not only to express the emotions that haunt us, but also to share with the people who have yet to find out that these feelings are alright, and true, and that it is so important not to deny them or hate ourselves for them. Because even as I'm typing this, David has sat down at the computer next to mine to write an essay of his own. And as he does so, I feel a surge of love and appreciation for him. And I know that this is *not* an occasional feeling.

DANIELLE, 15, MILFORD, CONNECTICUT

For as long as I can remember, the feelings I've held for my sister Paige have been less than loving. These feelings include anger, embarrassment, sadness and disappointment. I cannot remember the last time I thought to myself, "Wow I really love my sister."

My sister, who is now 13 years old and 2 ½ years younger than me, was born perfectly healthy with no complications, illness or any indication of a disability. That healthy baby was brought home and would change the lives of my parents and mine forever. One night while the Librandi family was enjoying a nice, quiet night at home, suddenly Paige was not breathing and unconscious. While my father was giving her CPR, I could do nothing but watch and feel total helplessness. Paige had "died." I don't know whether I was happy or sad because little did I know what would come next. Paige had lost the use of the left side of her brain, causing her to lose the use of the right side of her body. She was later diagnosed with Cerebral Palsy, a disability that requires her to practically live in a wheelchair and uses a special machine that talks for her. My sister, in my opinion, was next to nothing. She was helpless. Within the next thirteen years she would face more obstacles than I could ever imagine. Countless people would stare, make pointless comments and worst of all, pity her. I would yell, stare back and correct them on their ignorant views on people with disabilities. She has gone through numerous surgeries to help her just to survive. She has made the best out of situations that seem to have no light. In two years she will join me at my high school as a freshman and now after thirteen years of living with her, I have come to the realization of how much I love her and how I would do anything in the world for her. I love Paige with all my heart. And for those other brothers and sisters who feel that they hate their sibling and feel that they just make life harder, stop and think: Family is all you have and I would take mine over anything, especially her.

JACQUI
The Life of a Special Sib

How do you summarize the life of a special sibling, a person whose brother or sister has special needs due to medical problems or a disability? Two words do it most for me: worry and acceptance.

My worrying began when I was 13. My first sibling had been born only six months earlier, the sibling I had spent my life begging my parents for. His name was Eddie, after my dad, and I was only somewhat disappointed he wasn't a girl. He had a full head of hair and smiled often, giving a "shriek of joy" when he was really happy. I knew my mom had begun to worry about a month before because Eddie wasn't sitting up by himself yet, although his doctor kept insisting that it just took some babies longer and refused to think on it further.

What came after that, going to a neurologist for a second opinion, tests, and eventually a diagnosis, I don't remember much. It has been forgotten due to what followed.

Eddie received the diagnosis of Pelizaeus-Merzbacher Disorder (PMD), a leukodystrophy or neurological disease in which the myelin sheath around the brain and nerves is not complete—a very short and simple explanation for something that is anything but. Those with PMD do not have a strong immune system, which led to Eddie's first hospitalization at about 10 months of age.

Eddie caught a common cold, however not everyone knows that within the common cold another virus, Respiratory Syncytial Virus (RSV), can be found. For most people, catching a cold with RSV in it really means nothing, but for young or premature babies and those with a bad immune system, RSV can be fatal. Eddie spent a few months not only in the pediatric intensive care unit, but also in isolation. He had

IVs in his head, and six tubes going through his chest to his lungs because both lungs had collapsed, and he slept through most of it.

My aunt came to live at our house to take care of me and make sure I got to school, dance class, and the hospital. My parents lived at the hospital with Eddie. Occasionally my mom came home to sleep, or my dad to shower before work, but someone was always there with Eddie. He was never alone.

This was only where the worry began. You would not know this unless you have had to use one, but hospitals have a small room with some couches and a phone, which is saved for families without much hope. We spent several nights in that room, in tears. Most of our family was there, my aunts and uncles and grandmothers, but I was the only child and didn't understand how any of this could happen. When I looked at Eddie, I remembered how much he liked being held and swung around, how cute and happy he was all the time. We would never fully get those times back and I could not believe they were saying he could be gone from us so soon. I tried calling a friend from the hospital to talk about it, but she had never been through such a situation and did not fully understand, nor could she really understand what I was saying through my tears.

One night, the doctors told us we should say goodbye before they tried an emergency blood transfusion that might not save him. It was the worst night of my life. But Eddie has always been a fighter. He made it through that night and kept on fighting until he made it through the RSV. His first birthday was celebrated with the other children staying at the Rehabilitation Institute of Chicago. My aunt still lived at our home and my mom stayed at another aunt's who had an apartment in Chicago so that someone was still always with Eddie.

However, this was still only the start of the worry. As we learned more about PMD, we were given a life expectancy of three to five years. We were told of a yearly conference with the doctors studying PMD in Indiana. This was to become our family vacation every year. The first year we received a look at things to come. We were the sixth family to start attending the conferences and met other families with PMD boys, all requiring a wheelchair, and none the type of brother I had thought I was getting.

As the years began to pass, we would soon see Eddie have the worst symptoms of the boys at the conference. We would spend much of our lives in the hospital, Eddie had his own "spot" in the intensive care unit; it was always the same bed. We were able to keep RSV away, but not pneumonia. He would get a g-tube, which goes to his stomach and is how he gets food because he can not swallow correctly and if he takes food by mouth, it can go right to his lungs. We began to celebrate small miracles, such as Eddie staying out of the hospital for a full month.

He then received a tracheostomy, which is another tube, this one in his neck, going to his lungs. This helped him not only to breathe better, but to allow us to get the mucus out of his lungs easier, which leads to a lot less pneumonia. Now we were happy to celebrate two years of remaining out of the hospital.

Through all this I worried. I worried about Eddie constantly, I worried about my parents, and I worried about myself. I worried when we took Eddie out anywhere because we had to take this suction machine which gets the mucus out of his trach while making a very loud noise. I worried that this previous worry made me embarrassed of my own brother. I worried because I often felt Eddie was a burden and then felt guilty about such thoughts. I felt so many conflicting things and then worried that they were bad feelings or thoughts and so worried that I was a horrible sister.

I never told my parents how I felt and did not know anyone else who would understand. I worried when I asked for anything from my parents, I worried when I went out with my friends because my brother would never be able to do the fun things I did, and I worried when I was with my brother because I did not always know what to do with him. I worried when I actually made time to watch my brother so my parents could go out and have a little life again because I was convinced something horrible would happen while they were gone, and I worried that I was no longer as important to them.

I spent a very long time feeling like a bad sister and worrying about everything. The worrying did not help anything, either. Eventually I tried to distance myself to escape the worry and be normal again, but I could never escape it and only hurt my brother more.

LINDSEY, 17, ARIZONA
Being Zach's Sister

My big brother Zachary was born with Spina Bifida causing paralysis from the waist down and secondary health problems due to nerve and brain damage such as learning and emotional disabilities, bladder dysfunction, and vision impairment. He had five surgeries in the first five weeks of his life —another twelve in the next twelve years. He has used a wheelchair since he was in the fourth grade.

Two years after Zach's complicated birth, I was born. The only thing wrong with me was a single closed tear duct that just needed to be coaxed open with a pencil eraser. That was about it.

I was naturally a tough little girl, refusing to be messed with by my big brother. If he did try anything, it was common to see me dragging him by his big white curls across the room despite his delicate little head. His disability was invisible to me as a little girl. He was just my big brother and his realities were my realities. I remember meticulously detailing his crutches as I drew my family because his crutches were just a part of him and deserved to be featured in the drawing like anything else.

As years past, my mother devoted her life and studies to understanding her son's disability and the environment he would be faced with, eventually becoming an expert and even an advocate for disability awareness and rights in the community. She was even responsible for organizing an entire national conference in our city, coordinating events for hundreds of people with Spina Bifida and their families for three days. I look back on this now with affection realizing it was a reflection of my mom's commitment as a parent. But at the time, I felt it was utter discrimination against the "normals." There certainly was not a single "abled persons" conference that I had heard of.

As the sibling of a disabled person, I felt like the unloved one at times. During the latter part of my childhood, my brother's disability was all *too* noticeable. We were raised so differently. When we were teenagers, this glaring disparity was just "unfair!" Not only did he have my mom's undivided attention and concern, but he got to be on TV shows for disability awareness and showered with pets (assistance dogs) and new toys (crutches and special bicycles to increase mobility). When we got in trouble, I was sent to my room or grounded, while he was not. Not fair! But what could my parents do? It was not a punishment to ground my brother.

He *enjoyed* sitting alone in his room. We were two different people, who necessitated two different childrearing styles. When I was young, this just didn't make sense.

On the flip side, it wasn't until many years later that I learned of my brother's jealousy for *me*. Even though I was younger, I got to date first, drive a car first, had more friends, and did well in school. He hated me for the things he couldn't do, for the friends I had, and for the awards I got. But, at that time, I interpreted his anger and jealousy as "meanness" which made even less sense because he was so adored and pampered. There were years of intense jealousy, competition, and animosity between us.

Publicly, I was never ashamed of him or his disability. I didn't see his disability as awkward or difficult to understand. There were just certain things his body couldn't do—and so what of it? In school, I remember feeling sort of proud that I could relate to him and know all the details about a disabled person when others felt so awkward and curious about it. I felt like I had a special secret or advantage. However, when I was in high school, I did have trouble explaining medical supplies and the strange smells around the house. I was used to all this, but it made others raise their eyebrows. I generally opted not to invite my group of friends over spontaneously because of it.

Now Zach has graduated from college and I still have a semester left. During the past four years, we've had the opportunity to live away from home, to travel abroad, and go to college studying our different interests and passions. We've learned a lot about who we are as independent people apart from each other. We get along very well when we share a space no smaller than a college campus. (It should be noted, however, that our college campus has the distinction of being one of the largest in the country!)

I still feel like I'm less easy on him than my parents. I refuse to clean up after him and I expect a lot out of him—I expect him to do all that he is able to do. After all, he is my *older* brother. The problem is that I think he is able to do more than other people think he can. I don't have any emotional need to nurture him and take care of him like the rest of our family does. I have never pitied him. Sometimes I'll refuse to do a chore or favor for him that I wouldn't hesitate doing for anybody else because I'm so afraid he'll capitalize on his disability and become eternally dependent. There's still that little tough kid in me that won't be messed with. I always think, "He HAS crutches, why should I be one?" But the truth is that I sometimes wonder if I really don't know how fragile he is. Maybe he really can't do some things by himself.

He has a job and his own apartment now. I try to see him about once a week or so—not to see if he needs anything, but just to hang out. He takes the bus to work and somehow manages to get groceries, so I don't worry about him. He likes to go places with me if the bus can't get him there. Sometimes he asks if we can go to a dance club sometime, but I deny him those trips not because I don't know how to dance with a guy in a wheelchair, but rather because the guy in the wheelchair is my brother. I think he understands that distinction.

Just recently I had an eye-opening interaction with him that was an interesting comment on how our relationship has matured over the years. We were getting into my car to go to the store and I was disassembling his wheelchair, huffing and puffing to get it all piled into my little car. I must have let out a little sigh of irritation because of the energy required to do it over and over again. He asked sort of timidly, "Lindsey, is it a chore to be with me?" My heart sank and I was embarrassed about my sigh. I had to be honest with him, and told him that it *did* take a lot of energy to take him places, and that there are some days when I just can't do it. Then I told him I wasn't hanging out with him because I felt I had to, but because I loved him and he's the funniest person I know—truly enjoyable to be with. The interaction was significant because in previous years, his fear that he was a chore or a burden would have manifested itself in anger and fighting. My limited patience and energy would have likely reared its ugly head in the same way. But, in that moment of honesty, we were able to put those things to rest.

KIRSTEN, 35, PENNSYLVANIA
My Experience with Richie

I was babysitting and it was around 1:00 a.m. I was surfing the channels desperately for something to watch other than infomercials while I waited for the parents to come home. Exhausted, I stopped when I came across the image of a group of young children playing but they had no hair. I had seen kids like this before and I had never understood what made them look the way they did. As I watched I learned that these children had leukemia and were very sick but that they were also very special. I couldn't stop watching until finally the parents came home. It's funny looking back at that night; I think God must have put that show on especially for me.

The next morning my brother, who had had some routine blood tests the day before, for what the pediatrician thought might be mono, was suddenly being rushed up Yale New Haven Hospital. It was the weekend and it seemed like he never came home after that. I also rarely felt like a teenager after that. My mom had an antiques business and had been running a booth at an antiques show that same weekend. Suddenly at the age of 17 I was selling antiques by myself amongst grownups more than twice my age. I remember being scared; scared of having to run my mothers business, scared because my brother was up at Yale University Hospital and no one would tell me why, scared because suddenly it seemed like I had to be in charge. I ran the booth the whole weekend, and packed it all up when it was over. I had to, there was no one else to do it.

It was at the end of that weekend that my mom came home without my brother, sat us all down, and with tears in her eyes told us that Richie was very sick. He had a disease called leukemia and she wasn't sure if he was going to be okay but that we had to be brave. All I remember is thinking "NO!" I didn't have any one definitive thought other than that. I remember taking a walk and crying and running and crying. What were we going to do now? Later I remember thinking, "I guess that's why God put that show on for me so that I would be prepared for this."

You are never prepared for a moment like that. One of the biggest lessons I've been left with is that anything can happen to anyone; you are never prepared. You are never invincible. Life as we knew it was never the same.

There were so many emotions flying around from that point on. My parents were never home and I felt more responsible than ever for my siblings. If my parents weren't both at the hospital my mom was there and my dad was at work. Someone had to try to ask how everyone's day was. Someone had to make sure that if mom forgot to pick up someone that they got home. When mom ran out of gas on the highway because she was so tired and stressed that she forgot to put gas in the tank, someone had to drive it to her. My dad worked in NYC. So I had to be that person. At least that's how I remember it. I don't think that I had a choice in the matter; it was my responsibility.

There were other things that I remember feeling during that time . . . being angry at the kids who had been so mean to Richie when he started 9th grade because the doctors said that cancer can sometimes be brought on with stress . . . "they caused this!" . . . I remember always being afraid when Richie came home for a visit that he might fall and he'd have to leave again because he might hemorrhage . . . I remember feeling like my mother favored him and my yelling at him to stop looking for attention because he was sick . . . I remember being so angry that my parents were thinking of keeping me at home to go to college and all I wanted to do was be normal and go away . . . I remember feeling so guilty that I wanted to go away . . . I remember being so glad that Richie lived long enough and was healthy enough to make it to my high school graduation . . . when I went away to college I was always so glad to be away. . . it was so sad at home . . . everyone tried to pretend to be normal but we all knew differently.

I knew I needed to be brave for my brother but I didn't know how to act around him so I wouldn't make him worse. I was so mad at the nurses who tripped over his broviac and thought nothing of the pain they just caused him when he was already in so much pain. I hated that the hospital became such a familiar place that I accidentally kept referring to it as the hotel. I saw my father cry for the first time and I didn't know how to make him feel better. It seemed like my mother was so mad at me all the time and I thought I was being so helpful. I couldn't understand why it wasn't good enough. Every time the phone rang . . . FEAR! Was this the call? Was it the end? It was a very hard time, very stressful and out of control. But, I was always thankful that I got to say goodbye to my brother, more than once . . . but I will always feel so guilty that I was not there with him the day he died.

I know that my parents tried to make things work the best they could and having children of my own now, I don't know how they did what they did. I guess it just becomes a way of life that you don't even think about, you just do. I think I was just holding on the best that I could . . . I guess that's what they were doing too.

I have three children of my own and I worry every time they're sick for too long, their temperature is too high or they have to have blood drawn, that this could be the time they tell me one of them is very sick and there is nothing I can do about it. These things are in God's hands. We can try to do what is humanly possible but if He wants us, He is going to have us. One day my oldest daughter's pediatrician said he would like to have blood work done because she had been sick multiple times in a month. Immediately my heart started pounding. I asked reluctantly what he thought it might be, praying that he would say it was nothing serious. His response was mono. "Oh," I thought, "That's okay it's not serious." Later that night I awoke out of a deep sleep as if I had woken up out of a coma and remembered that Richie had been tested for what they thought was mono. I don't think I rested until I spoke with the pediatrician the next day. He started out by talking about the white cell count . . . "NO! Not the white cell count . . . when they talk about that it's never good!" Before he could go on I told him that I needed him to understand that I may seem a little anxious but this all hit too close to home, and I needed him to tell me: Is there any chance my daughter had leukemia? I couldn't wait any longer . . . I had taken a walk that morning and had prayed to Richie, my official guardian angel, "Please ask God to not make my daughter my lesson. I get that He's is trying to make me see that I haven't been concentrating on what's important but please, if He needs to really teach me, please let it be with something else besides my daughter." Then I prayed to God himself. I hoped that between the two I might get a pardon. I guess Richie had some pull because thankfully she not only didn't have leukemia but she didn't even have mono.

I, like all people, get caught up with the day-to-day craziness that is life. I do, however, stop longer and think harder when I have certain moments like this in my life that I don't think would have fazed me before Richie got sick. I think I am more sensitive to people who are going through something difficult and I also know to never say "I know what you must be going through," because I know from experience that you never really do until you've gone through it yourself.

I may be scarred in some ways from the experience but I do feel, even if it has taken some time, that I am better off having lived through it. I know that my brother is in a better place playing soccer with our dog Winnie and smiling down on me. I am thankful to him for going through all he did so that I could be a better person than I was before and maybe appreciate the little things in life a lot more. He is an angel.

We want to offer the support that our children need in times of stress. Often we need help ourselves in order to be able to guide our children. Sometimes our children guide us. Ultimately we learn so much from them when we listen. We learn about ourselves as well as the world because they view the world with untainted views. Yet children will get angry, and this is where we need to give them exercises to enable them to express themselves.

Often there is a loss that leaves residual guilt for not being there at the right time. As parents we do not recognize all of the things that children hope for or need in stressful situations. They do not understand why they cannot be at the bedside of their sibling at important times. We cannot always have the children there when we struggle to balance our emotions and time with each child. It is significant to realize the importance this is to the children. They grieve the loss of that time together.

Chapter 4

ISOLATION AND EMBARRASSMENT

❦

*"I always felt different from the other
kids in school only because when someone asked
how many kids were in the family
I would have to explain the whole ordeal."* —MEG

*"When I did start going to school again,
it seemed like no one really cared what happened."*

REMEMBER WHEN YOU didn't have the shoes your friends had? Or were you ever embarrassed because you could not go to the same movie your friends were going to? Or maybe you wanted the same game as your friends and you could not have it? Well now think about what it would be like if your family was different from everyone else's family. You sister or brother is sick and every one knows it, sees it, and looks at you differently. This is really not fair to children. And they never asked to have this happen. It just did.

When there is a sick child in a family, others may look at you like you are a different color. You feel separate and isolated from the rest of the world because your lives are different. All of a sudden things are dictated by the necessity of having to tend to one child who requires more help. The repercussions can be significant for the sisters and brothers in these households.

Isolation can be both psychological and physical for children. They can cut themselves off from family and friends to protect themselves from feeling "too vulnerable" or "too angry" to be with other people. They are now different from their friends, and most of their friends do not understand the ways in which they feel separate from the others in their class. Their peers get more attention from their parents and do not need to be so very patient. They are embarrassed and ashamed that their lives are like "not having the same shoes," only worse.

Children in families with a sick sister or brother are being asked to behave in a way that is not normal. There is often an inability to find a safe place to deal with the internal chaos. They are being told, "be good," "be quiet," and "not now" when all children need to be naughty and loud, and think they should "have it now." The expectations to be a perfect child force them into their own world that is safe. It is important that we see and hear these special siblings before they hide from the outside world and retreat into their own private world, along with their fears. This behavior—an effort to protect them from feeling too vulnerable or angry—can cut them off from family and friends

The result is that they escape into watching endless hours of TV, surfing the Internet or sitting in their room listening to loud depressing music. They may be too overwhelmed to do homework but continue with a numbness each day not knowing how to feel normal.

These issues can impede their psychological childhood development. At the Faculté de Médecine in France, in a study of families who have a child with cancer, it was noted that adolescents with cancer retreat into their own world and are not able to rebel in a normal age-appropriate way because they are dependent upon their caretakers. The impact on the sisters and brothers can be great and varies according to their age and the ability of the parents to adapt to the situation.

Adults, teachers and other caregivers need to be proactive in assisting with the isolation. If it continues for too long it will have a long-term effect on the child's psychological growth. They should tell the children that they care about their feelings and encourage them with words of praise and support. Letting the children know that you understand will provide them with the help they need to stay integrated with others.

Although we like to discourage isolation, we encourage quiet time without escape mechanisms. By learning how to find peace in solitude we are able to face our feelings with courage and with honesty. This is difficult in our world today as we are bombarded with information, noise and commotion. There is real emotional release, peace and calmness from prayer and meditation. It is important to use our time alone to work through feelings. Most individuals do not appreciate the value of quiet time. It enables us to develop answers to our questions and gain inner peace and strength.

No longer considered foolish or insignificant, hospitals are now beginning to realize the importance of spirituality in healing our body and soul.

David Larson, MD, a psychiatrist and president of the International Center for the Integration of Health and Spirituality has studied the impact of spirituality on health and coping with illness for over twenty years.

Dr. Larson said, "Even though we've had a wonderful technological advances, we've forgotten about how patients are feeling emotionally, especially those with chronic diseases. The more serious the illness, the more important the spiritual factor seems to become."

What many families do not realize, as they go through their experience, is that there is a community of families throughout the world who are healing everyday. There is an awakening appeal to support these families who are often isolated and tired of the challenges they face. With understanding and the power of communication within each of us, we can evolve into stronger individuals so that we can help other families through our common experiences.

Support groups can now be found in most medical settings for these special siblings that encourage discussion and offer relief. Children reach out to others within this safe setting while the group leaders encourage their verbal expression among them. Constructive exercises, such as writing personal journals to open their thoughts, help with this isolation; drawing brings development of new creative thoughts, and singing encourages positive mental states. All of these activities initiate uplifting mental thoughts and help to bring people out of hiding.

It is important for adults to discuss with children the relevance of how a unique experience, although hard, enables you to grow. Through time and acceptance of their difference, the isolation will melt away and an inner peace will grow. In reality, everyone has something difficult in their family. Some things are more obvious than others, but everyone has something hard to deal with. If you look at these as opportunities to grow as a person, acceptance is easier. When we search for a quietness within ourselves, our isolation dissolves and peace gently slides into our consciousness. With a gradual moving in a positive direction we learn to enjoy happy days again.

MEG, 14, NEW CANAAN, CONNECTICUT

My brother's death didn't shock me. I was sort of used to him being gone all of the time and seeing him sick, lying in the hospital bed. My family was always separated. Mom at the hospital, Dad at work, Kirsten in college, and Jim at private school. Mary Jane was the one I saw the most of. We were not too close when we were young because we are only two years apart, me being older.

Rich and I bonded a lot. We were the closest in the family, I always thought. Kirsten and Rich were always close, too. Rich was the first boy and had to set an example for Jim. Then he died all of sudden, Jim was the oldest boy. His role model was gone now and he had to set an example for me. This is why Jim and I become so close I think, I always looked up to him, he was so cool. Before that, I thought the same of Rich. I thought wow, he is so old and cool, and I want to be just like him.

We would talk all the time and hang out together. I knew most of his friends. There was a certain bond between us I cannot explain. But when he got sick, we sort of lost that bond. I was afraid to look at him because more of his hair might fall out or he might be too weak to smile. I always wanted to cry when I saw him because I felt so bad for him. Now that I am the age he was when he died, I can't even imagine living at the hospital while your friends are out partying or hanging out. I know he felt left out and wanted to live his life. It was like his life stopped as a freshman in high school while everyone else's continued. It wasn't fair.

When I gave my bone marrow to him, I thought, "Wow, now I get some attention." I didn't even think of the pain he was in. I just wanted to trade places, now I look back and realize what a hard two years he had and wouldn't want to trade places for the world.

After Rich died, I always felt different from the other kids in school only because when someone asked how many kids were in the family I would have to explain the whole ordeal.

I would feel pressured and the spotlight would be on me. I didn't know how to explain and I wanted to cry.

I always wondered what it would be like if Rich were still alive and he never got sick. Our lives would be totally changed. My brother Jim and I became really close when we started driving to school together in the mornings. If Rich were alive, would that relationship with Jim have been different? Would I have stayed close friends with Rich if he were at college now? Would we be in a different town? I think I would be a totally different person. I needed something to do to get my mind off of Rich, so I started swimming. I now go to Nationals every year in the spring. Rich made me a stronger person. I am not saying his death did any good, I am just saying he taught me how to stand up for myself and how to be strong. "Don't let anybody push you around." That is why my family thinks I am so "tough."

I really do think about Rich every day, though I think about what if he would appear to me from heaven and talk to me? What would I do? Would I be scared, happy, and nervous? He told me before he died that whatever I think he is saying to me in heaven, then he is saying that, and we can have conversations whenever I want. I still do that. I will have a conversation with him about a problem in my life, friends, and advice. I feel he is actually talking to me and I know he is there. Sometimes I know he is in the sky, then a minute later, right next to me. I always say goodnight to him and tell him I miss him. I know he is my guardian angel, like I am protected 24 hours a day.

I don't remember much about Rich being sick, but I remember sitting with the nurses playing games and waiting to go home. I hate hospitals and everything about them: the smell, the feel, the sound and the surrounding of sick people. I feel sick inside when I go there.

I know Rich will always be there for me and answer all of my questions. I am lucky that I could experience such a thing that could change one's life in the blink of an eye, yet, I feel this whole ordeal was a mistake and God wasn't supposed to take him.

LISA, 18, ANSONIA, CONNECTICUT

When my brother Mike was young our house was under construction. Mike has autism and one day he gave us a real scare.

We were in the middle of adding on to the house. We had removed one of the windows that used to be in his room and covered it with a large sheet of plastic. Because my brother liked to wander, we had locks throughout the house that he didn't know how to go through. Well, one morning my mom went to wake him up but couldn't find him. She looked all over the house and his room but he was still no where to be found. Even though she knew he didn't know how to un-lock the door, she thought the worst. She was about to call the police, when she heard his humming. She decided it was coming from his room, so she went in there but she still couldn't find see him, but the humming was getting louder. She finally found that he had taken down the plastic covering and climbed through where the window used to be. He was sitting inside the wall humming and was very content. Well, after that day, she boarded up the window to prevent this from happening again.

When you live with someone with autism you can have unusual things happen, but it doesn't matter as long as they are okay.

AMANDA, 17, EAST HAVEN, CONNECTICUT

My brother Brandon is almost 15 years old and has Down syndrome and autism. He is fatally allergic to nuts.

I remember last year my mom had decided to take a trip with some of her girlfriends to Florida. Something she hadn't done since before she got married. While she was on her flight to Florida, my dad had gotten a call from Brandon's school saying he had an allergic reaction and an ambulance was now on its way. My dad had just dropped off my friend at her house after our exams at school when he got the call. We hurried to his school and they were just getting ready to load him into the ambulance. Only one person can ride with the patient, so I went in the ambulance with my brother while my dad followed in our van. That short ride from his school to the hospital seemed like an eternity. If my brother ingests nuts his throat close and he can't breathe. His teacher shot him with an Epipen which helped open his throat. When we saw him before he got into the ambulance he looked fine, he didn't want to be held down.

When we got to the emergency room Brandon just really wanted to leave and he didn't like the doctor touching him, and he tried to jump out of the hospital bed a few times. It turns out he was fine and may not have even had a reaction at all. As scared as I was, I could not imagine how scared my mom must have been so far away.

ANONYMOUS, MINNESOTA
The Life of Cancer

When my brother Connor was two he started to experience the life of cancer. My family had to go through things like having to change his port every day, it was really hard, but there were people who felt sorry for us and sent flowers and gifts to us. He finished his treatment when he was five and there was no more cancer in him. But when Connor turned six the cancer returned. One morning my mom Julie and my dad Perry had to take Connor to the Children's Hospital in Seattle. After school my best friends Cindy, Torrey, Barnabli came to pick me up. When I got in the house, my parents called and told me that the cancer had come back. I hung up the phone and started bawling. I was staying at my grandma's house for about a year and a half. They were fun to stay with but I still wanted to be with my family. I would write e-mails to my mom and dad every day.

Every weekend I go to see Connor. Most of the time he was glad to see me, but some of the medicine that he had to take could make him grumpy. Sometimes he would throw major temper tantrums, but I always knew that he missed me. The medicine that the hospital gave him was very nasty. When Connor came home one time I tried some of it and it was way worse than the taste of wine. After a couple of months we started staying in the Ronald McDonald house. My family made a lot of friends there. Most of the kids had cancer and were also going to the Children's Hospital. Since we had been going to Children's Hospital so much I had memorized how to get to my brother's room and how to get to the playroom, cafeteria, gift shop and pool. Have you ever heard of "Make a Wish"? The patient makes a wish and they make it come true. It was Connor's turn. First he wished for all of the Japanese Pokémon cards in the world. But my mom and dad convinced him to wish for something else, so he wished to go to Disneyland, Knott's Berry Farm and Sea World.

When we got back to Seattle, we rented an apartment to stay in. The kitchen was really small and the bedrooms were small too. One night at the hospital my dad came up to me and said Connor was dying, and I felt like I was going to break in a billion pieces. A couple of days later he was dying and my mom and dad asked me if I wanted to hold him before he died and I said no because it was too hard. So I went back to the apartment and when they got home I asked them if he was gone and my mom said yes, that he's in heaven now. When I was in bed my mom gave me Connor's beanie baby, Angel, and she said that he would want me to have it. I grabbed it and started to cry. The same night, we went home to Anacortes, Washington.

I didn't go to school for at least seven weeks. My class sent me a card saying they were sorry about Connor. When I did start going to school again, it seemed like no one really cared what happened. When I walked into my classroom nobody said anything. But then the next couple of months I stopped talking about it. But I still felt like my life had been turned upside down and put into a tiny ball. I am trying my hardest to survive without Connor, but it is so hard. I thought, why did this have to happen to me?

And that is the Life of Cancer.

TARYN, 11, NEW YORK

My best friend in this whole entire world is my sister, and to live life with her ill and can't do many things changed my world, my life! To live life with an ill person is not easy! A lot of times you feel that your parents give more attention to the ill sibling and leave you out, and let me tell you I felt like that a lot! It does not make you feel any better! It changed me emotionally also because seeing all of what my sister has been through makes me have a second thought on life. Life is not fair, seeing all of these kids at Sloan Kettering in all different age groups fighting to survive is so unfair. You have to always think positive because you don't know what God's plans are.

I feel different from the rest of the world because all of my friends' families are fine and well, while mine isn't. They are never going to understand what we have actually been through. They are never going to see what I see, they will never know what has happened in my life! Yes, they are aware of what happened, but if you haven't experienced this, you really can never understand.

What I would like to tell others to make them understand how it feels is having an ill sibling is just as tough as being the ill sibling. You have to live with your parents switching every day to stay at the hospital to be with your ill sibling, not seeing your sibling every night, all the attention that the ill sibling receives, going to school not seeing your sister wondering if she is going to come home and be ok. Everyone would ask how my sister was doing. Rarely did anyone ask how I was doing. Life is not just tough for the ill sibling, it is also tough for the other sibling(s).

How it makes me feel:

· I am not more afraid because I have a strong faith and believe in God.

· I believe I am stronger because I have learned so much from my sister's illness and all the other children and their families. It has given me the ability to believe in myself and to help other people.

· I was angry at first because it changed our family. So much attention had to be given to my sister so that she could get well and I wasn't allowed to visit her because I was only

7 years old. I had to stay with friends all the time and I missed my family. Most of all, I missed my sister being well, happy and hanging out with me.

· I am more confident because I am able to share with others what happened and I know that my life is special.

Yes there are many things that came out of this. I met Christy Carlson Romano; went to Disney World; I got to meet a lot of new friends who are in the same situation at Camp Sunshine; and the Northwestern women's lacrosse team became part of my family when they adopted my sister and me. Even though things are bad there is always a plus side and you have to look for the positive things all the time! Meeting and doing all of these things makes me think how appreciative I am.

This experience changed me on how I look at the world, how I learned that life isn't fair. This was a lot for me to handle when I was 7. It probably would have been hard for me to handle now at age 11, too. If my life were a book and I read it before this happened to me, I probably wouldn't accept this or have wanted this to happen. I would just run way from it all! This experience made me be a stronger person, it made me know that I can handle anything as long as I just believe!!!!!!

This, most definitely, makes me lead my life differently. It makes me lead my life differently because I have a unique outlook of the world and I know now that life will never be fair because there is nothing certain. That is why it is so important to be happy and live each day with love. I am glad I learned at a young age then later! What God gives you, you must accept and never complain. God always has a plan and you have to have faith.

What I would like to tell others how to deal with this situation is you can always cry. Sometimes you feel so helpless and you just want to cry, and it is ok to. Also talking to someone about how you feel my help. If it is your mom, dad, aunt, uncle, whoever it may be, it helps.

This experience had an influence on what I do today because I have a different outlook of the world and to always give more than I should take. Some people need more than others!

———

It is important to remember that children need to have us acknowledge that they are feeling different from their peers and often isolated from the "normal" world. While taking note of the stress pressing on the family and the other children in the family, we should acknowledge that it is also a learning process for everyone to recognize that we cannot create a perfect world. Life will give every one of us challenges of one sort or another. Look around you and see that everyone is created with his or her own personality and looks. We are not supposed to have the same life as our neighbor.

We have also become confused about this point because of the media. The vision of what our lives "should be" becomes skewed through intense marketing in every shape and form. They attempt to persuade us through our senses, our eyes, ears and scent; buy this product and you will look younger, see this movie and you will be energized, take this trip and your life will be transformed. And yet, while some of this may be true, we all have to accept the reality that most of us will not be the most attractive, the most athletic or the most popular. When we accept our differences we gain strength and find inner peace. This, too, holds true for more difficult challenges like our health.

Chapter 5

SADNESS AND
HELPLESSNESS

❦

*"Daddies are not supposed to cry and
Mommy is not supposed to looks so sad."* —KELSEY

*"I find it hard that no one understands what
it is like; I find it really upsetting when Mum
has to go away because the hospital
where he has his operation is far away."* —JUNO

IN EVERYONE'S LIFE there are times of sadness where we
are upset by what is going on around us or in our thoughts.
These changes can bring us uncertainty, helplessness, and a
fear of the loss of happiness. Children experience sadness
when they do not get what they think they need or want. Sadness is even more intense when you are isolated from your
friends because of an illness.

A sick child within a family leaves a permanent imprint
upon the lives of the family members. Children juggle their
emotions to find a resolution to the unwanted feelings. Most
of the time we want to avoid the feelings that bring us away
from happiness, but when we learn to accept sadness as one
end of a range of many feelings, we appreciate the times
when we are hopeful and joyful. During emotional times, it is
helpful to learn about the power of detaching and letting go,
especially when we are sad and our lives seem out of control.

By accepting our sadness, we can let go and trust the lessons that life is trying to teach us. But dispite our trying to let go we will live with what happened.

In the book, *A Charge To Keep*, by George W. Bush, he writes about his sister's battle with leukemia, "I was sad and stunned," he says, "I knew Robin had been sick, but death was hard for me to imagine. Minutes before, I had had a little sister, and now, suddenly, I did not. Forty-six years later, those minutes remain the starkest memory of my childhood, a sharp pain in the midst of an otherwise happy blur."

We live in a country where everyone searches for happiness and we yearn to be happy all of the time. The media and our ever-increasing affluence as a country feed our expectations. If we were happy all of the time, it would not be real or normal. We would not be experiencing a life that would enable us to grow psychologically. In trying to understand our sadness, we can move towards the other side of feelings. By releasing the negativity we can welcome in a sense of peaceful surrender. In accepting our sadness we begin to understand that we cannot control everything in our lives. There will be times that will bring us disappointment and the emotion of true loss. In realizing that this is part of life, we are able to evolve into a peaceful embrace of what we are given.

Illness is not something that is welcomed and it can bring intense sadness. When we concentrate on the reason we are sad, we begin to overcome this very deep emotion and we learn and grow. We know that when a loved one is sick it will change our lives either for a time or forever. We do the best we can to improve the situation. It is often in trying to find resolution to our sadness that we are immersed in growth.

Although feelings of sadness must be felt when we acknowledge that someone is sick, it also can be brought into a state of acceptance. We start with sadness, move to understanding, then to mental acceptance and eventually to serenity.

Sometimes people experience depression when they are unable to deal with their sadness. When the reason you are sad becomes exposed, we can learn which feelings need to be "surrendered" in order to embrace the change, and accept what is happening in our lives. We might try saying to ourselves, "This has happened; I don't like it, but I must accept that it is real." Our minds adjust to the reality and we can grow by the understanding that we cannot change everything that happens to us. With maturity we accept that bad things will happen, and will bring sadness and helplessness.

We live in a world greater than each of us, and within that world we are meant to grow and accept many things that are difficult. We must not let these things impede our growth. This acceptance will allow us to be stronger and more balanced. Then we gain a sense of comfort and support from those around us.

JUNO, 9, LONDON, ENGLAND

I am Nine years old and I live in London with my Mum, my Dad, my older brother Cato who is eighteen years old and my older sister Tyro who is fifteen years old.

Cato is disabled and has to go to hospital quite a lot, it is quite annoying when mum has to be there for him and cannot pick me up from school or from swimming. But Cato is really, really nice and we get on really well. He does not get annoyed. Sometimes he lets me sit on his knee and drive his electric wheelchair. I find it hard that no one understands what it is like; I find it really upsetting when Mum has to go away because the hospital where he has his operation is far away. It is really scary when he feels ill or he is choking, but he is always ok. Cato is very brave because of all the operations he has had and he never is that scared and does not complain. It is hard being the youngest, and sometimes I feel he gets lots of attention, but it must be hard for him that he can not do everything that I can do. He always tells us to calm down and that he is fine. I am really lucky to have such a nice family who always help and sometimes I feel lucky that he is not worse and he is always getting better.

SOPHIA, 10, CONNECTICUT
Journal Entry 10/18/04

When my family really changed is when my brother Zack got cancer. I remember when the doctors weren't sure if it was cancer or an infection. My parents were still very upset because there was a chance he could have cancer. Tears poured down my parents face and mine while we thought about having him fight cancer once again. Zack had to have chemo too. During it, the effect was throwing up. He hates it so much. The whole summer went to a waste, besides helping my brother out; that was worth it!

Now this whole thing is almost over. On October 29, 2004, my brother will get surgery to get the tumor out. But then he has to recover. That will probably take a while. But otherwise the surgery is pretty soon and Zack won't have to take any more chemo. That is awesome! We are nervous though because the surgery might go wrong.

Journal Entry 12/15/04, now 11

It is not almost over. Still going on. I feel sad because my brother got cancer for a second time. I feel sad and lonely because he had to go through this and I was not with my family and not with my brother. But the people that I was with kept me going. I also felt pressure because when he got MRI's I had to worry about things like is his cancer gone. I also felt angry because it is like why did it have to happen to him! I felt different because this tragedy has changed my life. And not everyone has a family member that has cancer. It is also like Zack gets so many things from the society like gifts or money and I get nothing. When the society gave something to the family it is always my parents and not me. It is sort of like I'm never part of the family when they said family. But I also feel really lucky that my brother is okay now and that we got threw this safely. Also because we could have family and society there for us supporting us when we needed it. I am lucky that my family took me and fed me at that time. I would probably thank my Uncle Tom and Aunt Bonnie. Also my grandparents, Vivian and Joe, and my cousins and my Gigi.

KELSEY, 14, WAYNE, NEW JERSEY

An eight-year-old girl should be surrounded by boundless hope, never-ending dreams that seem could one day come true, and of course, Mommy, daddy and little sissy. At a mere glance, the truths in the real world could change a small child's life forever. For most of it was just an age when throwing dirt at the boys on the playground was fun and worries were never present. For me, being eight was a time that will always be a memory that lingers in the back of my mind. Many live lives as if they will have forever; I don't. I live as if each day is my last and I don't take much for granted. Being eight has left an imprint in my heart as vivid and irreplaceable as life itself.

I was a normal girl, smiles and laughs, cute and extremely loquacious. Yet, did the boy sitting next to me know that my little sister, Maggie was diagnosed with cancer last night? What is cancer? Why is her cancer called Wilm's tumor? Do I have cancer too? Do people really die? What's it like to die?

Walking into school that week was difficult. I was a deer, being hunted by the eyes of fellow students who seem to be equipped with the guns that would shoot me down until I cried and slowly slipped out of view. Their eyes hunted me, never leaving me alone. I felt that people knew more about cancer than I did. What is cancer anyway and why does Daddy cry at night? Daddies are not supposed to cry and Mommy is not supposed to look so sad. I felt tears evacuate from my eyes as my emotions slipped out from my reach and into the hands of my fellow students.

Where is Maggie? Daddy said she is at the hospital but what is that and why am I crying now too? I was scared and the world seemed to cave in on me as everyone stared at my pathetic tantrum. Did people feel the weight of my tears running down my cheeks as I did? They were the thunderstorm and I was abandoned, lost, and being rained on in the dank darkness. They consumed me and I couldn't see anything but this mysterious "cancer."

My dad took me to Hackensack Hospital for the first time that week. I was too young to understand where I was going and too afraid to ask why. The hospital was bigger than a New York City skyscraper and cleaner than a whistle! As I walked past the gift store, I saw a boy without hair. Where was his hair? That's when it hit me. Maggie was sick, just like that boy, and I was soon to find out how sick she really was.

Life seemed to pause for a brief but dragging period of time and I still easily cry if the word cancer is spoken. The hospital was my new second home, yet not a comfortable one.

My dreams seemed to have wings on which I would fly away from the doctors, chemotherapy, x-rays, and sad faces of parents whose little boys had no hair just like the one I saw in the gift shop. My mom saw how much I was trying to execute the hospital out of my life, so she brought me to a group to talk with a social worker and other children so that we could have our questions answered at group. I finally knew that Daddy was crying because Maggie had cancer, a very bad sickness that could cause death. I learned early in life what the meaning of death was and also what the meaning of life is.

I met Chrissie at a sibling support group. Chrissie was always wild, and I was quite the "little animal" myself. We took every moment and made it fun. It was our way of facing the ugly face of cancer and finding fun in a time that was so full of confusion.

One day Ellen, the support group leader, asked Chrissie how her little sister was, as she did everyday (and as she continued asking everyday). Chrissie began screaming things I had never heard from her usually sweet, fun mind. She threw a fit and then quietly slipped under the table to hide from the truth. I also got mad at Ellen and joined Chrissie under the table that served as our safe haven.

Up until that day, Chrissie was very brave. Now she was acting like a true eight year old, something we had grown out of long ago. We had matured through the experience and were aware of our own maturity level and that of peers around us. It was civil war, but we finally came out from hiding and Chrissie told our group that her little sister was dying, probably by Friday evening. I didn't know how to deal with this so I said, "NO, she won't, I will make sure she is okay, Chrissie." But I can remember the relief I gave to Chrissie through that foolish statement that spilled aimlessly from my mouth.

Friday came, but Chrissie didn't come back. Little did I know she never would. Ellen told us that her little sister had passed away that morning, prior to "group." That was when I stopped laughing, stopped smiling. I even stopped dreaming. I had already been forced to grow up rapidly and now the only truth I knew was being sucked from me like a vacuum. Just as Chrissie's sister was gone, so was my innocence and therefore, I was no longer that child that I was supposed to be. I was blind, deaf and mute, all at once. I learned more than I wanted to know; I learned little children could die, too.

Time, years, months, weeks, days, hours passed and my sister came out of chemotherapy and my mom stopped crying. My dad stopped looking so dead, and life was beginning to feel normal again. I was more mature than my friends that year and ever since I've felt the power of my actions and works. I feel each moment and I know that life is precious and random things can happen day to day with out any sense of reason or explanation.

My main flaw now is that I act too seriously sometimes and people find it hard to understand why. I wish I could tell them why and how I grew up so fast and was far more mature than they were now when I was only eight and they still had their dolls and dreams. Just as Chrissie's little sister was taken from her and so many people I met at the hospital were taken from their families, my innocence and childhood was taken from me that day at group. Since then, I have never been able to look at a hospital as a building. I see blood, chemo, death, bald children and most of all I see my childhood being taken and my new matured self-emerging from the entrance.

KATHARINE, 12, MINNESOTA

My brother Will is a cancer survivor. He has been through a rough road, but he is healthy now, thanks to the nurses and doctors and the Mayo Clinic. That's not it, he's had cancer TWICE!

When he was sick I always felt sad and worried about him at school. But when I was at the hospital and he was there, I knew he was in good hands. One thing I loved to do there was play in the playroom with Will. I felt tired or sometimes energetic when I would get good news.

Sometimes you feel different from the world, but most of the time I think there are always other people with the same kind of illness so you don't have to feel left out or scared because you can know that your brother or sister isn't the only one out there.

Most of the time I am scared because there's something that could always go wrong, right out of no where and your brother or sister could be gone forever. But Will is always here with me and I usually don't worry about it. I am confident and I don't fret but know that at this moment he is probably feeling great.

The second time my brother got sick wasn't nearly as bad as the first. It was all because his tumor was about the size of a pencil eraser. But in Kindergarten, when he first got it, it was much bigger. He also got cured much faster in 3rd Grade. I feel happy about that.

In 2005 our family got to go on a Make A Wish trip! We went to one of the best places . . . Disney World. We went over Christmas. That was the best. The weather was awesome, about summer temperature. We stayed at the best village ever. There was free ice cream and pizza whenever you wanted. The food was awesome. All of us went to every theme park. My favorite ride was the Tower of Terror.

This summer we got to go to Alaska for Hunt of a Lifetime Trip. Wow, was that amazing. In all we caught 250 lbs of fish!! There is so much to say about it.

All of this sickness made a whole new me. Now I look at everything differently and am thankful for what I have.

I am so glad that my brother is well and I thank God for it every day.

KATARINA, 7, FAIRFIELD, CONNECTICUT
Anything is Possible

I think anything is possible when I look at my brother. He was born with cerebral palsy. They didn't know if he would stay alive. They didn't know if he would talk or walk. He had many opursashns (operations). He didn't walk until he was 4. He needs a lot of help. Now he is 12 and he plays baseball. He bowls and he is a boy scout. He trys very hard at everything he does. He does better now than he did when he was little. He loves to do stuff but most of the stuff he wants to do he has to work harder at it than everybody else. That's why I think anything is possible.

————

The most important thing we can do to move from sadness and helplessness to acceptance and growth is to realize that everyone has things that happen to them that make them sad. We think about what it is making us feel this way, spend quiet time accepting what we cannot change, and contemplate how we can grow from the challenges we are faced with. Gradual peace will come upon us as if we are maturing and growing. This will enable us to move forward towards happier thoughts.

When someone we know is in such a state of mind, we can help them out of the feelings into a place of understanding and acceptance as well. This is a positive thing that we can do for anyone. Children will begin to accept the difficult things more quickly if they hear that we, as adults, also can be sad and frustrated with our feelings. In spending time talking to children we will transcend their isolation and fear. When we realize that we can overcome sadness, the world seems easier to live in.

Chapter 6

GRADUAL UNDERSTANDING

"If he were alive today, I would like him to see my Walter Schalk dance review, and one of my lacrosse games, and how tall I have grown." —MARY

"My best friend in this whole entire world is my sister, and to live life with her ill and can't do many things changed my world, my life!" —TARYN

THE SIBLING NOW sees the reality of what has happened to their sister or brother. They enter a new understanding: "Oh, I see what has happened. I may not like it, but I see it. I understand that my life is changing. I will be fine. I will be okay."

Things begin to change as siblings start to embrace life on realistic terms by learning to accept the lessons that are part of life. This often leads to spiritual and emotional growth. By accepting responsibility for their thoughts they can begin to use their emotional tools of journaling, art and writing to open up to others. The exercises in this chapter help them to focus and take charge of their emotions. Change occurs because of the healthy outlets of letting go of negative feelings.

Comprehension of our lives depends upon how we see each day. If we get up every morning and see a beautiful day, then the things that occur during that day are not overwhelming. Our thoughts and emotions precede our happiness. If we see life as good then we can tackle our daily challenges more easily. Knowing that we are not alone in our thoughts is in itself a wonderful thing. When we discuss our thoughts with others we reach out to find support and this then gives us a framework to solve any issues that may impede our happiness.

The sisters and brothers of children who are sick need to talk with those they trust to develop a structure of relationships that allow them to build a new- found happiness. This strengthens the awareness that there is a world beyond their own life, one that deals with issues that are greater than theirs. The individuals in their lives, family members, siblings, classmates and caregivers will support them because of the trust the children have given them.

We need to reinforce the idea that life will go on and they can have a normal childhood. They may need to fit other things into their day to accommodate the sister or brother with special needs that their friends may not have to experience, but they can do that. Their lives can be happy and they can do normal things like other children; there will just be restrictions in how things are done each day.

Once children begin to acknowledge that they are part of a bigger picture, they mature and evolve. Then acceptance and understanding of what is happening becomes easier. A gradual acceptance of their family—with all of the challenges that comes with that family—becomes part of who they are. It will eventually shape who they are as individuals. This does not need to be determined on any particular day, but once accepted, will be part of the growth and maturity of the child.

When we look at the beauty in each day and see the positive in our relationships with our friends and family, we learn to be grateful for all that we have. We all need to make a point to look for the goodness in our own lives from the break of the day to live a fulfilled and peaceful life. When someone is sick it is easy to concentrate on the illness and what it is doing to our lives, but by accepting the illness and by looking for the goodness in each day we will find understanding. This will lead to resolution in our thoughts and a peaceful acceptance of our life.

MARY JANE, 12, NEW CANAAN, CONNECTICUT

I never knew Rich all that well, but the really good memories stick with me, memories that I could never forget about my brother. I think more about him today than I did five years ago, but maybe that's because I'm older now, and think of dying as something more serious than someone just leaving, and never coming back.

When my mother came back from the hospital that day, Jim, Meg and I came scampering into the living room in our socks to hear what she had to say. Jim was listening most intently of all, as we all received the bad news. Mom let out the sadness through tears those last days, as she seemed to know Rich was going to die. I would ask her why she would cry, and through her tears, she always had the time to explain it to me in a way that I would somehow understand. She would say, "We will all go to heaven one day, and Rich was picked by God to go first."

After Rich died, things seemed to change. We all got older, and had gone through something other families had not. I personally thought it was okay for Rich to die because of all the stories of Rich in England, and at New Canaan High School. He seemed to have a great life. At family dinners and birthdays, stories would be told about Rich and Jim stealing candy bars, missing subway trains, and beating up Kirsten, our older sister. These stories only seemed to be told after Rich died, to make us remember him in a good way, not the way he was in the hospital all those months: sick with a fever, hooked up to an I.V.

The memory that I remember most of all about Rich is in our first house in New Canaan, sitting on the white bench outside on the patio, eating oranges with him, and Winston, our dog, whining at our feet for a bite. Rich had no hair, but he was wearing a hat. This is the memory I think I will remember the longest. I don't know why I do, but for some reason, I like it.

While Rich was sick, I became good friends with the nurses of section 7-4 of Yale-New Haven Hospital. When visiting Rich, I would snack on Saltine crackers and apple juice, while Mom would talk to the doctors about Rich's condition. One day, while Rich had to rest, I wanted to see him. I was in the hospital unit alone for some reason, while the nurses watched me. I asked to go into Rich's room, but they said I couldn't. I cried and cried to go in, feeling abandoned and alone without his quiet, yet comforting demeanor beside me in the same room, yet they told me that I couldn't. After that, I appreciated seeing Rich whenever I could, even if he beat me at playing Chutes and Ladders on the hospital bed.

If Rich were alive today, I would like him to see my Walter Schalk dance review, and one of my lacrosse games, and how tall I have grown. After writing this story, I guess I do know Rich pretty well, but not as much as I would like to. I don't know how he got as far as he did after getting leukemia, but I will always be proud of the success he did make, and hope he is watching over me today.

MAX, 8, CONNECTICUT
About My Brother, Ari

Ari was born on 1992, April 21. When he was the age of 4 he had a stroke. He was in the hospital for six months. When he was in the hospital I called him "Little Indian."

When he finally came out he forgot everything. Very slowly he learned everything all over again. Now at the age of 10 he still has difficulty with some things and half of his body is so very weak that he can hardly move it. It will always be harder for him, but he can do still many things nobody on earth can do. There are some things he can do that I can never get close to achieving. He'll always be my brother. Whoever tries to push him around, they will be answering to me.

Special words from Max:

· You should never laugh when people have difficulty because they can do something that you can not do.

· God, thank you for giving me everything I need, especially my brother.

· Thank you God for all of the miracles you do, especially my brother.

· Thank you God for saving my brother from dying.

MALLORY, 13, ORANGE, CONNECTICUT

At first, he appears to be normal. But if you really get to know him, you'll see that he isn't. He keeps me up at night laughing hysterically for no reason at all. His walk is weird, as far as walks go, I suppose. He hops up and down when he plays video games. If he wants something, anything at all, he gets it. He has autism and ADD (Attention Deficit Disorder). He's my little brother, Cameron.

My parents always tell me that Cameron is pretty normal. But he really isn't. Yes, Cameron is high-functioning (which means that he has a normal IQ). But that doesn't mean he's normal. My parents like to think he's normal, but that's just because they're his parents and he's their son. From my perspective, it's very different. They don't realize it, but my parents treat Cameron (and my little sister) way better than they treat me. It's unfair, because they get to do a lot of things that I wasn't allowed to do when I was younger. For instance, they recently saw the Indiana Jones movies. My parents would never let me see them until last year!

I always wish that my life could be normal, but it isn't, and I can't do anything about it. Cameron will always be Cameron, unless a miracle cure is found. Even if one isn't found, I'll still love him, no matter what. That's what sisters are supposed to do.

KATIE, 11, GROVER BEACH, CALIFORNIA
Evan, the Brave Boy

My brother Evan is in a wheelchair due to a birth defect. He was born August 27, 1987 and is now six years old. We found out before he was born that he had a birth defect. My mom always had to go to the doctors for tests. We found out he was a boy and gladness filled our hearts until the day we found out the bad news.

Evan would be born with something called Spina Bifida. When he was born he would have a hole in his back that looked like a half a bubble tAT would leave him paralyzed from the waist down. Another thing Evan would have was Hydrocephalus. This means there is too much spinal fluid in his brain. To take care of this, Evan would need to get a shunt. This is a tube going to the abdominal cavity, which is where your stomach and intestines are.

The day before Evan was born my mom and dad went to UCLA medical center. My grandma came to stay with us. It seemed like forever before the big call came on August 27, 1987. The baby had been born.

We were very excited and happy. Evan had to stay in the hospital for 17 days after he was born. When the day of his arrival came we made a banner. The banner said, "Welcome Home Evan."

I think I was more excited to see my mom than Evan. When he came home there was a bandage on his back and head. It was on the head because the doctors had to do surgery to put in the shunt. There was a bandage from the hole. He looked so tiny and cute.

When he first came home Evan stayed in a little crib, which was in my mom and dad's room. He was finally big enough to sleep out of my mom and dad's room. He shared a room with John and David. When he was two, he slept on a mattress that was on the floor. I would go underneath the bunk bed that John and David shared when Evan was not in the bed. When he was three he got his own bed he has now.

Evan wasn't just in the hospital when he was born. He has been in the hospital three more times. The first after his birth surgery was to get something called a stoma. Since Evan couldn't feel when to go to the bathroom the stoma helped him do that. The second time he was really scary. On Christmas day Evan got really sick. He kept on throwing up. By the day after Christmas, Evan was in bad shape. He kept on throwing up, and he got dehydrated. Evan had to go to the hospital for something called scoliosis. That is when your spine is curved. He was in the hospital for eight days.

There is one more sickness Evan has that I have not mentioned. It is a kidney problem called Renal Tubular Acidosis. He is on two medications to stop that problem. His kidneys don't fill properly because of too much acid in the blood. The medications do help, but Evan doesn't always want to take them. The first medication he does okay with because it tastes good.

Evan learned how to walk when he was about 2 ½ with leg braces and parallel bars. Evan was almost 3 when he got his wheelchair. Unlike the other things that Evan uses to get around with, he seemed to know exactly how to use the wheelchair. Evan can walk with a walker and leg braces connected to a back brace from the scoliosis. He also can get around in a stander. It is the same thing as a wheelchair, except you stand in it. Evan is strapped in so he won't fall.

Although kids with Spina Bifida can't use or feel their legs, their arms are very strong. Evan can do stuff nobody in our house can do. He can lift his whole body up with only his elbows on the floor. Evan weighs about 25 pounds and for a six-year-old, I'd say that is quite an accomplishment. Evan is also a good pusher. When he tries to push someone he really uses his arms.

Every morning Evan goes outside and waits for his bus. The bus sends him to Chris Jeperson School in San Luis Obispo. This is a school for only disabled kids. Our goal for him is to go to Grover Heights Elementary School in Grover Beach for the first grade next year. Grover Heights is our neighborhood school.

I don't know what my life would be like if Evan wasn't with a disability. He has helped me understand about kids like Evan. He also inspired me to do my best like he does. Evan has really changed my life as he learns and grows happily and pushes his disabilities out of his way.

GOOD DREAMS
A poem by Katie

Today I dreamed that Evan walked.
He stepped on his feet,
No longer ill, and no need for a wheelchair,
Today he stood tall and proud.
My brother ran a race with me,
And when it was done, he had won.
His legs, no longer limp, had life.
He seemed to gleam with glory
At his win, his wish comes true.
Maybe someday, not far away,
Not in dreamy fairy land,
He will no longer need no help to stand.

MIRACLE ON WHEELS
A song by Katie

I want to tell you that I love you,
Even though I think you know.
You are my little angel
Watching me here below
And I don't know how your
Heart can fit inside
Your tiny frame.

CHORUS:
You might be the smallest one
But the love in your heart is so great,
You are my miracle on earth
Dissolving fear and hate
You are my miracle on wheels

I want to tell you that I love you
You mean everything to me
You are m little angel,
The way I came to see
The Love and Light that comes
From inside your tiny frame

I want to tell you that I love you
In your chair and RGO's
You are my little angel,
Your heart just grows and grows
Even though your legs have
Stopped working, your heart
Is strong inside.

REPEAT CHORUS

I want to tell you that I love you
I know you love me too.
You are my little angel
I know this to be true
You made me see the boy
Inside your heart
Full of Love

REPEAT CHORUS

I want to tell you that I love you
You are my miracle on wheels

JUSTIN, 12, MASSACHUSETTS

Living with a sibling that has had brain cancer is challenging at times because he needs more help than we do. I feel sad for him. Every day I feel the same.

This experience makes me feel different from the rest of the world because a lot of people in this world don't know what it feels like to have a brother that had brain cancer. But I am not angry. I have a wonderful loving brother. But I'm more afraid because we never know what could happen.

I am stronger before because I have gone through a difficult phase in my life that has made me stronger. The one good thing is that my brother is safe and healthy. Our family helped each other through this horrible time.

It changed me to be more cautious of my life and other peoples' lives.

Yes, because if something happened to some other person then I would already know that experience, I could help them get through it. I would tell people just to take life day by day. It's not easy. They should take each day, slowly and help each other out and always think positive thoughts.

It has made me more kind to people and how I can be kind to a person even if they are not kind to me!

———

We learn to be grateful for all that we have by making a point to look for goodness in our own lives. We should teach kids how to look at the beauty in each day and in their relationships with friends and family. By doing this we realize that we can be happy despite having a sick sister or brother. While this understanding comes at different times to each individual; faster to some than others, it does happen. Sometimes it is faster because of maturity, and sometimes it is because of their innocence and ability to see things clearly.

When children realize that parents are not ignoring them, but that they are balancing everything in their lives, they will be happier. This brings a release of control issues when the siblings see the situation for what it is. Parents are going through their own transition, yet it is important for them to acknowledge the other children in the family when they make the step to accept life within the family. While everyone's life mostly revolves around the sick child, now they do not see it as negative, but rather *accept life as it is.*

Getting to this stage is so positive and the rest of the siblings' growth follows soon after. It is a time of release, patience, acceptance and maturity. Once this occurs, children acknowledge that there are others who also have challenging situations. They know they are no longer so very different. They begin to feel normal and they understand that every day can be happy again.

Chapter 7

REACHING RESOLUTION

❧

*"I am stronger before because I have
gone through a difficult phase in my life
that has made me stronger."* —JUSTIN

*"One thing we learned it's that
even when you end up in a very different place
than you ever could have expected,
it is still within all of us to make it a good place,
a peaceful place, and a joyous place. "* —EMILY

EVOLVING INTO A peaceful place, children come to understand that they cannot change the reality that one of their
sisters or brothers is going to live a life different from the rest
of the world. They have been chosen by God to have a family
that needs to view life differently. Most are fortunate to see
that there is a little silver cloud to it, including the ability to
embrace the uniqueness of their sibling. Their life may not
be exactly like every one else's life, but they see that life is
precious and not to be taken for granted. They accept their
situation as real and ongoing.

They do not necessarily feel that, if given the chance, they
would have chosen the differentiations of their family, but
they do embrace the fact that they are part of a bigger world
and they are not the only ones who face challenges. With the
knowledge that they cannot change the uniqueness in their
family, they can now talk about it in a more positive way.

They appreciate that they have experienced difficult lessons. There is a newly discovered strength and respect from within. Siblings can now find better ways of communicating with others and they take responsibility for their actions and emotions. It isn't that life has gotten easier or less complicated; it's that they are better at reacting to situations.

At this stage, siblings may not like what is going on, but they are not as anxious and frightened. Hopefully they have gained a wisdom and understanding of life that is more balanced. They have become more mature because of what they have needed to learn and they no longer think as children, but have a more experienced perspective on life.

They begin to map out their hopes and dreams and start to write down all of the things in life they want to accomplish. This brings a hope for the future by having a vision of doing something they love. They often view the world as if saying, "Okay, I know that this is the way life is. Now I need to accept it and make the most out of it." This viewpoint enables them to move forward. It gives hope for all that is about to come.

Having healthier reactions allows us to begin dreaming about easier times and less stressful days ahead. There is a new bright beginning in each day, once we look for it. Maybe it is a call from a good friend who cares about you, or a teacher who says you are doing a good job. It could be that someone asks you to go to the movies or have a bike ride with them. If you recognize these as bright things in your day, your whole attitude turns more positive and you will begin to enjoy the good that is in everyone's day. Sometimes we just have to look for it. Once you do, it becomes easier and easier.

LAUREN, 11, WEST HAVEN, CONNECTICUT

A couple of years ago when my sister was about two, we took her to Yale New Haven Hospital. She had a fever for a couple of days and my parents were worried. The nurse who saw us the night before had taken a blood sample. A couple of days later my mom got a call from the doctor. Later we went to the hospital. That day was the day we found out my sister had Immune Deficiency. Now everything is doing fine, especially my little sister. She is eight and after a long war with our insurance company, she got her infusion pump at home. Now we are all hoping for the best, happy life she can have. A tip for people with siblings who have any disease is to be strong, and tell your family and friends how you feel and they will help you the whole way through.

NICOLE, 22

When a child is diagnosed with a disability, it is bound to change a family's life. When my brother, Sean, was diagnosed with autism, my family didn't know what it was, let alone what to do. After realizing the ineffective treatments where we were located, we had to move to another city to give him the treatment he needed to live the most normal life that he possibly could. While this was good news for my brother, it meant turning my life upside down. I had to move away from all of my friends and the life I knew, during a difficult period in my life. I went through some hard times during my early adolescence. While I was angry and upset about the little attention I received from my family and my peers, I understand now that it was all for the better. I grew into the person I am today and I don't think I would be the person I am today if

Sean hadn't been diagnosed with autism. I wouldn't have met the people I met, experienced the wonderful things I have been through, and live the life I do, if it wasn't for him. In my mind, I thank him for that every day. He has also inspired me in life to be sympathetic to others who are less fortunate than I am. My heart melts every time I hear about a disabled or troubled child going through hardships because I've seen it firsthand, and we were lucky with Sean, because he wasn't as severe as most children are who are diagnosed with a disability. He's helped me grow more as a person, and inspired me more than anyone I know and will ever know.

KAREN, 17, ANSONIA, CONNECTICUT

My brother Mike has autism. He says funny things that make us all laugh almost every day. He is very special.

Okay, so one time my 15-year-old brother went up to me and out of nowhere said, "Karen, do I have a six pack?" Which was the most random thing he had ever said. So, I just busted out laughing and I said, "A six pack?" And he just stands there, smirking at me, so I decided to cause some trouble because I'm like that. So, I said, "No Mike, you have a keg. He did NOT want to hear that. He said, "I do not have a keg! Why do you say that I have a keg! Why do you say I have a keg! You are wrong! And this continued back and forth for like five minutes until I finally said to him, "You know Mike, maybe if you go on the treadmill every once in a while that keg of yours may turn into that six pack you want so bad."

So he just stops for a minute and thinks and he's like, "Oh . . .Okay. I will get a six pack now." So a few months go by and he keeps talking about the keg and how he didn't believe he had one. After a while, he started working out at school and he went up to me and insisted he doesn't have a keg anymore and to prove it he lifted his shirt and said, "It's not a keg anymore. But it's not a six pack. Now it's a pint." So, now my brother has a pint. He is funny.

EMILY, NEW YORK, NEW YORK
For Matt

My brother and I step to the edge of the ridge. Beneath us we know is the safe water of the reservoir, deep and full, that will catch our fall and buoy us to safety. But tonight beneath the trees that line the water's edge, it is dark, and even the full moon can't quite illuminate where the distance will stop and the water will begin. He'll go first. I know he will. He always does. And I will follow, because I always have, because that is what little sisters do.

We've danced this little routine on the edge of the ledge before. But no matter how many times we have jumped, like any big leap, you have to get yourself ready to go before you take the plunge. It's become more meaningful to us since my brother had been sick. When he is well enough, we've learned to savor the times when we're free to run through the woods again, to stand on the edge of the reservoir and throw ourselves into life. It's an appreciation we probably wish we'd hadn't been forced to learn so suddenly in our early twenties, but we savor it now, because in many ways we know it is the only weapon we have to fend off our fleeting youth, the loss of our benign innocence and the realization that all of a sudden, the world is no longer safe for us, our lives are no longer spread before us as a promise and there is not one, not mom or dad and not the doctors, who may be able to save us from the sheet of black ice that spreads out in front of my brother like a scene in a movie where you know what is going to happen, but you sit on the edge of our seat in denial and suspense praying it may not be so.

And so on this night, and others, with nothing else left to do, we jump. It feels like a long stand at the top looking down. No matter how well you prepare yourself for what it will be like, you are always shaken by how long you are suspended in the air, in time and in space before you hit the waters.

Once we're safe in the embrace of the reservoir I float on my back and lay my head back into the cool water until my eyes stare behind me just gazing over the surface of the water. At the right angle I swear I can see where the heavens above fold into the waters beneath, meeting at the tree line. My brother is swimming near me in the silent waters but even on this night when for this moment life is so vibrant in our young lives, I know there will come a time, perhaps sooner than I will expect, when this line between the stars in the sky and their reflection on the water's surface is where my brother and I will have to meet.

My brother and I still talk, although not as often as we used to. I attribute this to age and us going on with our lives in different directions, but this may just be a false comfort I tell myself to allow me to feel less guilty for my own laziness to reach out to him. And up over the hill in front of me, his lithe body is floating over the pavement as he runs the two-mile loop near our home, a navy blue t-shirt damp with sweat over his broad shoulders and his blond curls lightly bouncing on his head. Or there was another time when I visited the Columbia River Gorge to watch the windsurfers dance across the water, when I saw him bring his windsurfer to the shore and start walking towards me, a huge smile on his face and a hand raised to greet me.

Matt is of course dead. He died of cancer eight years ago

when he was twenty-three and I was twenty-one. I still wear several of his t-shirts although they are slowly becoming threadbare, and I still turn up the radio when one of his favorite songs is on, although I don't force myself to take myself back to his death while the music plays like I used to, like a personal memorial service every time Thunder Road pours from the car speakers.

He was running a mile thirty seconds slower at the end of the summer than at the beginning. Looking back that would be the only clue he might have had to tell him is body was turning on him. But rather than thinking of cancer, because what young athlete would think of that, he attributed this lag in time to the two week trip to Ireland with the Williams Soccer Team, during which perhaps he had celebrated good time with his best friends with one too many Guinnesses. His time would be still be fast enough to win the one-mile race on the first day of pre-season next week, something that was important to him as the captain of the team, and he knew he would close the gap as the season rolled on.

But the season didn't roll on for my brother, or not the way he had hoped. He would lead his team to their first national championship, but it would be from the sideline. Call it mother's intuition, but my sweet mom insisted my brother see our family doctor for a yearly physical before he returned to college for his senior year. And call it doctor's intuition but our family doctor on an instinct he would never be able to explain, ordered a blood test outside the typical routine for this healthy athletic young man before him in his office on a late August day. And faster than my brother could run a mile, my family was thrust into a battle that we never saw coming, that we were sure we could win, but that would eventually twist us around so many times that by the end of it, the family who started this journey would never recognize the one who finished it.

It's all a muddle in my head now, those long two and a half years when my brother was only periodically well and the many months spent in the hospital. I refuse to revisit them. Any family who's battled a terminal illness knows that while death can be a peaceful reprise, there is still very little that is peaceful about the actual dying, watching the changes and struggles and the simple loss of dignity that no one can hide from.

We would learn what it meant to be scared. My little sister and I would learn what it is like to see your big brother cry. And we would all learn what it is like to feel the fabric of a family unravel under the weight of a cancer that didn't just live in my brother's body, but infected us all. My father would be more realistic than any of us and we would resent him for his pessimism. My mother would hold us altogether for just long enough for us to say good-bye to Matt. And my sister and I, six years apart, would walk our worn path next to my brother. She would look to him as a hero and cherish the attention he gave to her while she was navigating the sticky days of middle school and he was home recovering from the most recent treatment. These days spent bonding over new TV shows and Hannah's first dates would forge a friendship between them that they never would have had if my brother, eight years older than little Hannah, had spent those years in college like he was supposed to. I think that is what people like to call a silver lining. There were a few of those.

Matt and I passed the long days in the hospital together. We knew each other better than any one else knew us, but the countless nights we spent talking in the hospital, as well as the two bone marrow transplants Matt had in which my marrow was injected into his bloodstream, left us more like twins than just siblings. I remember the night before the second bone marrow transplant; I visited Matt in the hospital and held his hand while he fell asleep. We held hands for so long that I could no longer tell where my fingers ended and his body began. At the time, I thought that was a sign that everything would be okay.

There were good times during those two and a half years too, even in the hospital. There were times when we would double over with laughter at something my mother did to make my brother smile. We'd remember the stories of our childhood: the boy with whom we carpooled who could never shut the door on the first try and walked like he had a load in his pants; the year we thought it was hysterical to make fake farts for the entire bus ride to and from school; the day Matt caught my best friend, Ned, and I hiding underneath my bed with a cigarette lighter we found down by the Lilly Pond; the time Matt negotiated a later curfew for the homecoming dance with the simple line, "But Dad, she is the hottest girl in school." There were times when we'd pass an afternoon idly listening to a John Grisham book on tape, or dreaming about the meals we would make for Matt when he could eat a normal diet again. There were times when even in the discomforting fluorescence of a hospital room, we knew that the warmth and love of family and the memories of a childhood well spent were more than many of us could ask of in a lifetime.

By the time my brother was gone, our family was very different. The largest difference was of course his absence, setting the table for four and not five, walking through the airport as a family with two daughters and wanting to scream to strangers, "There was a brother here once. It's not two girls."

I remember coming home from college after I graduated and waking up late on a Sunday morning. I could hear my mother downstairs in the kitchen, the faint sound of her friendly voice on the phone. And I heard my father's long stride in the hallway when he took a break from his work to refill his water glass. Then I heard my sister's little slippered feet shuffling out of her room. I lay in bed for what must have been an hour waiting to hear the cadence of my brother's footsteps hit the wood paneled floor outside his bedroom and thinking how different life would be if only the rhythmic thud of his stride were still with us. It's funny what you miss about somebody.

When the fist year without my brother was over, we all started to climb out of the holes we retreated into and come back to each other. In some cases the reunion of my family went well. My mom still cries a lot, but no one would know what to do if she didn't. My sister, with the help of her first love, saw the light of the world again and enjoyed her senior year of high school with relentless enthusiasm. She may never forgive God for what he did to her hero or allowing her to watch it happen but she, more than anybody, carries my brother's spirit in her life. She is quick to embrace new adventures and like Matt is boldly more willing to feel this world more heavily that most of us are able to. My dad tried to move on with all of us too, but there is one thing I think we all learned that year, which is that mourning the death of a brother and a son is highly personal and particular journey for each individual, and even in the closest of families and tightest of marriages, when it is over sometimes you can put the pieces back together and sometimes you can't.

My parents would eventually divorce, like many couples do after the death of a child. They could move on alone, but just not together. When I look at my family now, it is clear that we are changed beyond just my brother dying, but if there is one thing we learned it's that even when you end up in a very different place than you ever could have expected, it is still within all of us to make it a good place, a peaceful place, and a joyous place. What do they say? The broken heart still beats.

Matt taught us that. He taught us that enjoying the blue cheese dressing on just the right buffalo wing could be a religious experience, and that finishing a good book, taking an early morning jog, or pulling out of the driveway with Bruce on the car radio are all the little events that should make us all pause for the glory of this life given to us.

He spent the last week of his life in the ICU at Brigham and Women's Hospital. By the end of the week, eighty of his friends had joined my family at the hospital retelling the stories of his life. If we weren't in a hospital, you could have mistaken it for a party. My mom told stories of a young Matt being potty-trained, my sister and I told stories of obnoxious Matt farting on our heads, and his best friends told stories of misguided attempts to land girls and spring break trips down south. Even in the shadow of death it was a glorious week. Matt had always had a way of bringing people together.

It rained non-stop for those seven days as our friends and family, Matt's teammates from Williams College and a history of old girlfriends kept vigil in the waiting room. Then on that seventh day when the doctors told us solemnly we had to let his body go, the machines stopped beeping and, amazingly, the sun came out. As the rays fell through the Venetian blinds of the hospital window, casting themselves through the refractions of grief in the room, it was almost as if you could see Matt's spirit rise out of his beaten body and up to a place where he could run again, where he could dance and smile and where he could be free.

I know he is safe in heaven. I've never wondered about that. But sometimes it can be as simple as imagining that he lives on the other side of the country, somewhere gorgeous and clean and full of the outdoors, maybe Santa Fe or Taos.

Or perhaps he is further away, camping in New Zealand or snowboarding in Chili. I write letters to Matt in my journal. He'll of course never receive them, but somehow I think he enjoys them.

I know he visits me. Sometimes he shows up in a song on the radio, or the sun breaking through the clouds on my wedding day or when I fortuitously bump into one of his best friends on the street when I am suffering a particularly conflicting day. Eight years later as I sit here starting my life with a wonderful man whom my brother never got to meet, and expecting my first child, I still feel my brother with me. Like any big brother, I know he still protects me. One of Matt's best friends, Jen, is a gorgeous blond with a heart as big as her smile—a woman whom it is easy to understand why my brother loved so deeply—shared at his memorial service: "When you jump off the rock at the reservoir and you feel yourself plummeting through the air and then plunging into the cool layers of water, falling into the darkness until your toes graze the shocking mud at the bottom, Matt is in the force that pulls you back up again, back up through the dark layers through which you just fell until at last you break the surface and are safe among the stars again."

TYRO, 15, LONDON, ENGLAND

It is the hardest thing when someone in your family falls ill. Not only because you are constantly worried about them but because it pulls a massive strain over all of you. When my brother fell seriously ill, once again my whole world crumbled. The strong bonds that had always held my family so closely together were being pulled and stretched by the thought that they might lose one of their members. My mother, having been crowded by different doctor's opinions and test results all day, was exhausted every evening when she finally came home. She could no longer help me with reading my abbreviated versions of *Wuthering Heights* or by gluing various postcards for my school project; which at the time seemed very important to me. I knew what was going on with my brother, but was determined to try and keep everything as normal as possible. We all had completely different ways of coping with the situation, so it was impossible for us all to work together. And that's what's most important. The worst part was when I'd catch my mother rushing for the bathroom red eyed and hurriedly clinging tissues to her cheeks. I'd have to try and protect my sister who'd also start crying, while encouraging my dad to comfort mother because he is, by no fault of his own, not particularly good at those things, while I would desperately be wanting to burst into tears myself, and would also be feeling terribly guilty because the only person who wasn't crying was my brother, who of course had the most right to. At the end of the day, I think that's what got us all through. The strength and astonishing determination my brother showed everyday in hospital. Although physically he was the weakest, Cato will always be the strongest out of us all and it is this shining spirit of his which keeps us all together.

WELCOME TO HOLLAND
A poem by Emily

> I am often asked to describe the experience of raising a
> child with a disability—to try to help people who have
> not shared that unique experience, to understand it, to
> imagine how it would feel.
> It's like this . . . When you're going to have a baby, it's

like planning a fabulous vacation trip—to Italy. You buy
a bunch of guidebooks and make your wonderful plans.
The Colisseum.
The Michelangelo David.
The gondolas in Venice.
You may learn some handy phrases in Italian.
It's all very exciting.

After months of eager anticipation, the day finally arrives.
You pack your bags and off you go. Several hours later, the
plane lands. The stewardess comes in and says, "Welcome to
Holland."

"Holland?!?" you say. "What do you mean Holland?? I
signed up for Italy! I'm supposed to be in Italy. All my life
I've dreamed of going to Italy."

But there's been a change in the flight plan. They've landed in Holland and there you must stay. The important thing
is that they haven't taken you to a horrible, disgusting, filthy
place, full of pestilence, famine and disease. It's just a different place.

So you must go out and buy new guidebooks. And you
must learn a whole new language. And you will meet a whole
new group of people you would never have met.

It's just a different place. It's slower-paced than Italy, less
flashy than Italy. But after you've been there for a while and
you catch your breath, you look around . . . and you begin to
notice that Holland has windmills . . . and Holland has tulips.
Holland even has Rembrandts.

But everyone you know is busy coming and going from
Italy . . . and they're all bragging about what a wonderful
time they had there. And for the rest of your life, you will
say, "Yes, that's where I was supposed to go. That's what I
had planned."

And the pain of that will never, ever, ever, ever go away . . . because the loss of that dream is a very, very significant loss.

But . . . if you spend your life mourning the fact that you didn't get to Italy, you may never be free to enjoy the very special, the very lovely things . . . about Holland.

———

Sometimes it may seem strange that you can feel happy when something so hard is going on in your life. But you can and you should strive to find the light at the end of the tunnel. The tunnel in this case is our emotions. The light is the happiness that we are all meant to feel in life. A challenge does not mean that happiness ends. Maybe it will make us appreciate how good life can be. Most of the children we spoke with who had a sister or brother who was ill, felt that they now appreciate life more and enjoyed each day more because of the ability to see how precious life is.

Many people who do not experience these extreme situations are not able to understand even the simplest joys in everyday living. You can sing, you can laugh and you can dance. Be happy with what you can do! Children can creatively put their dreams into practice by imaginative exploration. Adults can join them in learning to embrace simple joys. It brings happiness to adults to refresh the experiences that invite peace. We must strive to see the little things, the best that life has to offer. We all have dreams, no matter how hard or easy our lives are. These dreams are meant to motivate us and bring us pleasure. If we embrace them we will find so much joy.

Chapter 8

LEARNING LIFE'S
LESSONS AND LOVE

⬳

*"Corrie has taught me to be more
caring and accepting, and through her I realized
that true beauty lies not in what is expected
but in the little differences in each of us."* —FARRYL

*"But through it all, while others in
the hospital were screaming away, you were
a quiet warrior."* —STEPHANIE

AS TIME MOVES forward, siblings learn the strength to defend their brother or sister. Now, feeling more empowered about their situation, they are better able to take them under their wing. What does it mean to know how to be emotionally protective of ourselves and others? What characteristics have we developed? Are we more courageous? Are we better at managing our anger and depression? Do we laugh more? Do we realize that we can become leaders by allowing our uniqueness to shine? Let's look at what are the best ways we can encourage dynamic thinking.

Commending the differences between people becomes part of the maturing process; it teaches tolerance. What is the lesson of tolerance? What does it ask from us and give to us in return to as gifts? If you were to teach people about the lessons of tolerance, how would we know what to look for in our own life that asks us to be more tolerant? Challenging experiences, such as having a sister or brother who is sick, helps us to view our values and appreciate the needs of others. We also learn how to define words like "normal" and "gifted" as individual terms, and we begin to recognize that others grow at their own pace.

There is a metamorphosis from the shock to the reality to understanding, resolution and protection as the siblings gain respect for their sisters, brothers and their parents. They also gain respect for the many complexities of the world. This evolvement of the emotions leads to maturity beyond their years and sets them into a world of emotional intellectual knowledge that can be beneficial to them in the future. The sisters and brothers know what it is like to wait and be patient. They must see the pain that the parents endure. This usually becomes part of their new personality and creates a desire to help others and be a support to those who are thirsty for comfort. Their personalities are stronger and reinforced by the life lessons given to them.

Determination to make a difference can come at a young age. Jace Richards was a 5-year old boy when he wrote a book with his mother, Donna Richards, to educate other kids about autism. Jace did not like it when other kids made fun of his younger brother who had autism. *My Brother's Keeper: A Kindergartener's View of Autism* was written to help children understand what autism is and how it affects children and their families.

These children often become protectors, healers and leaders as adults. They can see that life can be fragile, but that you can be strong. With this knowledge, they lean towards professions such as teachers or doctors or caregivers. They want to pass their new knowledge to others. This is one of the truly good things that come from learning hard lessons in this way.

Life is a journey. We all have our own path. Actually, it is very exciting to think that we are all unique! If we were all doing the same thing everyday, we would not be very interesting and no one would be inspired to be an astronaut or a wonderful chef or a nurse or teacher. Everyone has a destiny to be a productive and happy person, and each day's choices help you go down your individual path. What many people do not understand is how much we can work towards creating the destiny we dream of. If we decide to do something productive and positive in our life, we will be rewarded with great happiness and joy.

It is important for us all to realize this as we accept our challenges, it can sometimes be overwhelming. We need to ask ourselves, "What can I learn from this? How will this shape who I am and who I will become?" Through the consideration of the differences in our lives we are empowered to start our own journey. When we have admiration for others' journeys, we allow our family and friends to create their path. This is critical to who they are as well.

We will find the answers to our prayers in silence and peaceful thought and we will have the messages come to us. If every day you think positive thoughts and do positive things, even if it is just doing exercises for now, you will get the answers you are praying and waiting for.

COURTENAY, 26, SUMMIT, NEW JERSEY

I just couldn't stop walking. Though this was not the first time that I had felt so overwhelmed by embarrassment that I had to remove myself from the situation, I must say that this was one "Melissa incident," as we like to refer to them,

I knew I would never forget. I was in my early teens, probably 13 or 14, which we all know is a tough time in a girl's
life. This is the time when you want more than anything else
is just to fit it—like any other girl going through the same
hardships—acne, braces, and a misguided attempt at a perm.
With that in mind, imagine being away on my family's annual
summer vacation on Cape Cod—for a month! A month away
from friends at home, to spend time with the people who you
want to be with the least for 30 days straight and then to have
this happen.

This particular day began no differently than any other,
the weather was beautiful and after a hurried breakfast we all
went our separate ways: tennis, golf, sailing . . . until we met
up again for lunch at the Club. I remember this lunch as if it
were yesterday, not more than ten years ago; talk about something that will stay with me FOREVER! Just to offer a little
background, the "Club" is nestled in a quaint New England-
type town where more often than not, you will find stuffy,
uptight, conservative women who are there to "relax" while
their husbands commute from the cities on the weekends—I
know, what a life!

Aside from the beautiful views from the lounge chairs
on the beach, you can also take in the views from under a
shaded table on the patio above. Lunch was served from 11:30
a.m.–2:00 p.m. so needless to say, the patio was packed with
people the entire time. Finding a table was never an easy
chore so whichever family member was hungry first would
go upstairs and lay claim to the next available table, and then
call for the rest of us. That particular day it was my younger
brother, Andrew, who felt the hunger pains first so he walked
up the stairs to wait patiently by the patio for a table. Nearly
half an hour had passed when we heard Andy call our names
and we put on our shorts and shirts (you cannot eat on the

patio in your bathing suit) and the remaining five of us slowly climbed the stairs. When we finally reached the top and were walking towards the open table at the other side of the patio the "incident" occurred.

My sisters, Christine and Caroline and I were walking no more than five feet in front of our mom who was with our older sister Melissa, when out of nowhere we heard my mother gasp (which is something we have heard before so I knew it had to be bad). As I turned around, I saw Melissa leaning over the table of random strangers, grab a hamburger off one of the older women's plates, who looked like she has just walked off the tennis court from her morning round robin, proceed to take a bite as they all looked on in complete disbelief, and then threw the partially eaten hamburger back onto her plate. Imagine your reaction to this? Mine was pretty similar. As I stood there bright red, sick to my stomach with embarrassment with the sun reflecting off the silver that encompassed my mouth I could do nothing but turn right back around and walk away and act like this was not my sister. My mother, having dealt with these situations so many times, apologized profusely and insisted on buying her a new lunch. However, these women just wanted to be left to their whispers and wanted nothing more than my mother to remove this person who was blocking their sun and making them all uncomfortable. So she did, with tears in her eyes, she did.

Melissa, my older sister by 15 months, has Rhett-Syndrome, which is a neurological disorder, which in simple terms has left her functioning as a toddler. She understands but cannot do things for herself. For example, her vocabulary consists of single words. She cannot stay anywhere unsupervised; she needs to be dressed, bathed and her meals need to be prepared for her. The frustrating thing for her is that she understands what is going on the outside but cannot communicate back to us, which in turn makes her frustrated and causes her to act out in order to get attention. And, she does it in ways that definitely make us and everyone else who happens to be a witness stand up and take notice—and this "Hamburger Incident" was just one of many.

I am now twenty-six and have been through many stages in regard to my feelings about Melissa and her mental retardation. When I was very young I don't think I even realized that there was anything different about her. She was my older sister and I looked up to her. Young children can be mean, but I think that children are generally naïve to differences when they are young. It is a learned behavior to be mean and judgmental of others based on their imperfections. I became much more aware of these attitudes towards my middle school years when it was so important to just be "normal." This is the time in a young person's life where being mean can sometimes be cool—even though I look back now and know that it is just insecurity that makes people unkind to others. I must admit, I did my share of laughing at others who were handicapped, slow or just not up to our standards of perfection. How ridiculous! Even Melissa, my own flesh and blood was not exempt from some of the remarks. Though I would never make them myself, I would never say anything to anyone else who did because why would I want to be the one to stand out from the crowd? That is exactly what I didn't want so I let people make fun of mentally retarded people and, even though I felt guilty inside, I never said anything.

Thank God times change and with age (hopefully) comes maturity. I remember being in college; it was my freshman year. My mother had come down to see me at school and brought Melissa with her. As I was walking them out of my dorm I remember hearing these three "boys" standing in the hallway and laughing and making fun of Melissa as we walked by. The redness returned to my face as it once had and that awful feeling returned to my stomach. This time, however, it was not because I was embarrassed for my mother or myself. It was because their ignorance and lack of compassion stunned me. At eighteen years old, these three men could stand in a hallway and make fun of a handicapped person. It made me sick and from that moment on I decided that anyone I ever hear making a crude joke or any sort of derogatory remark about someone who is disabled, mentally or physically, will get an earful from me. Now I realize, the power lies in being a leader rather than a follower.

I count my blessings everyday that I am able walk and talk and function like a "normal" person, if there is such a thing. Whenever I am upset about things like a breakup with a boyfriend, a bad haircut or a bad day at work I try to remember that if these are the biggest problems I have I am a very lucky person. I can change things that make my life imperfect, unfortunately my sister Melissa cannot and through no fault of her own has to live rest of her life with Rhett-Syndrome. I guess the bottom line is . . . if she has to live out the rest of her life like this, why can't we all make it easier for her to do so instead of making it harder?

Many people do not know this, but even though she cannot say anything back she can hear and does understand everything you are saying.

STEPHANIE, 22, CONNECTICUT

Angela, I love you so much. I see the picture of me as a newborn coming home from the hospital. You were only four years old, but you are holding me so tightly in your arms with so much joy and love in your eyes. You were welcoming me into this life right from the beginning; you were welcoming me into the family. Even though I was too young to remember this picture, I can feel in my heart that you were there for me.

And you never stopped welcoming me. When we were little girls and your friends would come over to play, you always invited me to play along. Most big sisters told their little sisters to take a hike when the big kids came around, but not you. You always made me feel like I was welcome, like I belonged wherever you were.

We used to share a bed and stay up way past bedtime doing teddy bear Olympics with our stuffed animals. It was always you and me; we were an inseparable unit. Two blond-haired, brown-eyed little girls, we had our own magical world.

I looked up to you like you knew everything. I always tried to copy you, from the clothes you wore to the things you said, to the way you tried hard in school. I couldn't always live up to your perfectionist ways but I sure made an effort trying.

We knew how to make each other laugh. I remember making ridiculous noises and goofy outrageous 80s outfits. We always had a good time together.

And we could have a good hearty fight, too! Remember when I used to pinch you during all those long car rides and then tell Mom and Dad that you did it? Sorry about that . . .

We moved to different states and different towns. We grew bigger and older and became teenagers. But the fact that we loved each other, and were the best of friends, never changed.

I remember when you were diagnosed with leukemia. You were only 16. We were so worried about you. Thank God you were so brave and strong or else we never would have made it through. I never even saw you cry once in the two years you had cancer, and you certainly deserved to have a few good cries for all of the hell you went through. You lost your hair and gave yourself shots every night, but I never once heard you complain.

There was no doubt in my mind that you would get better. You were my big sister and you could do anything. You had always been successful at everything you'd done and I was sure that you could beat this too.

And then everything stated to unravel quickly. Hospitals, nurses, the transplant, transfusions, allergic reactions, rashes; you lived behind plastic. We couldn't even touch you, Angela. But through it all, while others in the hospital were screaming away, you were a quiet warrior. So brave. So young.

The day you died, Mom, Dad and I gathered around you and held you. I am not sure if you knew what was going on. We were telling you that we loved you and would always be thinking of you; that we would pray for you and that we'd all be together again, someday.

I guess the way you held me in your arms as I came into this world is the way that I held you as you left the world.

When I die all the pain will be gone when I see you there welcoming me to the other side, just like you welcomed me into this life. I can't wait for you to hold me again in your loving arms.

FARRYL
My Sister

"Hush little baby, don't you cry; Mama's gonna buy you an apple pie . . . " The soft whispers of a six-year-old's made-up lyrics swirled softly about the room. Her arm wedged firmly between the bars of the crib, she was content to weave rhymed words over the sleeping head of the little girl as she stood in her own pajamas; content to simply watch the little girl lie there. After all, she was sure it would only be a few short years before this baby would grow into the little sister she had always hoped for, a little sidekick to follow her around. It would only be a little while. She smiled as she tucked a blanket around the sleeping child and twisted her arm out of the crib. Only a little while before she had the sister she had always dreamed of.

The day Corrie was born will forever be ingrained in my mind. I had hurried home from kindergarten only to be whisked to my grandparents' house, where the news I had been eagerly anticipating for months awaited me: My mother had a baby! Breathless, I waited for the phone to ring, a million questions dancing through my mind. Would it be a girl or a boy? What was its name? Was it a sister? Finally?

Oh, how I hoped it would be a sister! I had spent long enough playing older sibling to my brother. After all, while I longed for a playmate to share my stuffed animals and baby dolls, he wiled away the afternoon dumping toy cars into piles on the floor. A little sister, I figured, would be there to share everything I did. She would join me as I played Barbies and dress-up, she would learn from me as I taught her to bang out songs on the piano and read. I could already perfectly envision the days we would share together.

Without warning, the ring of the phone cut through my thoughts. After being informed that it was indeed my father on the other line, I scampered anxiously to wrest the phone into my own trembling hands, unsteady from anticipation.

"Daddy?"

"Hi, Farryl . . . Guess what?"

I didn't detect anything strained or out-of-the-ordinary in his voice. If there was something unusual in the way he spoke, I didn't notice or simply don't recall. I was six, and I was beyond excited. All I cared about was the words he spoke next.

"You have a little sister."

My voice caught in my throat before I was able to choke out the only words that came to mind: "Excuse me?!"

In an instant, my dream had come true. The next few days flew past my eyes in a blurred excitement; a visit in the hospital, an exclamation of the news to my friends, the first time I so carefully cradled Corrie in my arms. The whispered words Down syndrome didn't faze me at all. To me, they were two meaningless words coupled together, bestowed for some reason on the perfect baby girl who was my sister.

Of course, time fluttered past—tiny first steps and first-word elation—and I began to realize that there was meaning behind those two words. Other kids didn't visit the special school their sisters went to. They didn't laughingly try to get their sisters to pronounce their names correctly; didn't cringe when they heard someone being made fun of. Other kids' sisters, after all, weren't placed aside, weren't labeled with terms that were set to define them.

But just as I learned why Corrie was perceived to be "different," I also understood that the label "Down syndrome" had no bearing on the fact that Corrie was still very much the sister I had always hoped for. Day after day, I'd bound into school with a new story to tell my classmates, and in time they saw Corrie in the light that I showered her in. My friends quickly accepted and embraced her for the cute little girl who happily greeted the world with a hug; my fifth grade class visited her school to share holiday gifts and play with her classmates for a few hours. Sometimes it took my peers a bit longer to look past the label, but I was glad once they finally viewed her as just another sister of one of their friends.

Like all sisters, Corrie and I have our own sets of jokes and traditions to keep each other amused. When I baby-sit for her we'll pop a bag of popcorn and watch Disney movies; we both have an uncanny ability to directly quote the same ones. I used to do her nails for her while we watched the Mets game on Saturday afternoons; now she knows all of their names and helps me root for them through the TV. At the same time, I remember constructing flashcards when she was younger of various words, laying them out on my floor, and attempting to teach her how to read. Yes, the process was not as easy as I had anticipated before she was born, but seeing Corrie's face light up when she learns something new is more rewarding than I had expected as well.

I've been asked if I ever wish that my sister were "normal"; if I ever wonder what life would be like. My answer is simple: since the day I first held her, Corrie has been the little sister I envisioned. We have our fights. We have our loving moments. We swap shirts or spoons of ice cream. Expectations have altered throughout the years, but the common theme of sharing our lives as sisters has remained. Corrie has taught me to be more caring and accepting, and through her I realized that true beauty lies not in what is expected but in the little differences in each of us.

"Hush little baby, don't say a word; Mama's gonna buy you a mocking bird . . . " The echoes of my six-year-old self still lurk in the walls of my house. Growing up with Corrie has transformed that girl—having a sister with a disability comes with both the good and the bad, but it has undoubtedly helped shape my own life. It's easy to look up the words Down syndrome and take the definition at face value, but labels don't even begin to explain the funny, caring person my sister is. Sure, somehow she always wins our family's games of UNO, but I'll take that if it means I have her as my personal cheering section at all school events. After all, I did indeed get my six-year-old wish for a little sister sidekick. I got Corrie, who lovingly informs me that everything from my hair to my outfits look "crazy" each time I leave the house, who puts on impromptu concerts for anyone willing to clap, who's perfectly content to wildly cheer for the Mets and Islanders with me. And that's the only label I'd ever give to Corrie: my sister.

EMILY, 11, MASSACHUSETTS

My sister, Lexie, is a brain tumor patient. Everyday I feel different. Some days I feel great and some days I feel terrible or scared. I think it depends on how my sister is doing. If something is wrong I might be scared or stressed or even mad. If everything is going well than I would probably feel happy and strong. Sometimes when something scary is going on I feel different and like no one could ever understand how I feel, but lately I've felt like I fit in just fine.

I feel more confident knowing that my sister has made it this far and that she's doing great now so I think and hope that from here on things will only get better.

Some good things that came out of this are that I met a lot of people that I would not have met if it weren't for this. And another good thing that came from this is that I got to go to camp sunshine, hole in the wall gang camp and a make a wish trip. Plus, I got the experience of being a part of SuperSibs.

Now I often think about how I can help other people not have to go through what my sister or I did or help them get through it. I think I understand unfortunate things that happen to others better too and I understand what they're going through or how they might feel.

I appreciate the good things that happen to my sister because of some of the bad things that have happened to her and other kids with cancer. I would like to tell others some ways to deal with this situation because I had some support and it helped me so I would want to help others too.

———————

Compassion and understanding are addictive and contagious. We learn by what we see. Children who experience love in their families know that their sister or brother who is sick or has disabilities are wonderful individuals and deserve more compassion and patience than others. Most often, these sisters and brothers become their sibling's protectors and guardian angels. You had better not "mess" with them or you will be told how they feel. Now the reality of the world is real to them and they know that everyone is different and, although they may not need special help in life, they are accepting of the fact that their sister or brother does, and they are there to help, too. The respect for life that these siblings have learned has made them stronger and often leaders in their worlds.

We live in a world where young movie stars are promoted for living lives of partying and taking drugs. This narcissistic behavior is encouraged by the media as being fun and adventuresome but it is very damaging to the values of American society. Those who must deal with the reality of having someone sick in their family must come to the realization that these stars have strayed from what is productive. They now know that these media stars are artificial, as they have forgotten what is important in leading a healthy and peaceful life.

Together with the help and love of family, teachers and caregivers, siblings can stay focused on who they are and where they want their paths to lead. Respect for life encompasses appreciation for others and high regard for oneself. This reverence grows though mediation, prayer and consciously thinking positive thoughts.

Chapter 9

DETERMINATION
AND FAITH

❧

*"Now I often think about how I can help
other people not have to go through what my sister or
I did or help them get through it."* —EMILY

*"Now I can truly understand that no matter what
kind of person you are, you can contribute to the world
in a number of extraordinary ways."* —LETICIA

*"To me, my life is one that is better than
anyone else is because it has changed me as a person
and I am thankful for that."* —CATHERINE

ALONG THE JOURNEY of emotional growth, these young
people come to the positive conclusion that they still love
their sibling and they express that love, despite the fact that
this special sibling is making their lives different from others.
They also understand the love of the parents towards *all* of
the children in the family. They express the strength of the
family.

Brothers or sisters with a sick sibling are often healed with
a strong sense of faith. Many of the children's stories we received show an intimate understanding that God is protect-
ing them. If the child died, there is faith that the child went
to heaven. They often express the understanding that they

will see their sibling again. How we practice our faith and what that faith gives us in return is often discussed with children in this stage.

They learn that through these experiences and adversity, there is a commitment to do good things with their lives. They now know how important the sick sibling has become in their life and they express how, with this human understanding, they are going to enjoy every day. A significant number of children express interest in becoming a professional who will nurture others. There is a sense of personal responsibility to make the world a better place and to comfort others. The siblings wish to share the importance of finding compassion and strength, now that they are able to keep a happy and healthy perspective despite the difficulties in their lives. There was a determination within them that is stronger than in most children. Their experience has shown them difficult times and they learned to accept it and made it a priority to make the world a better place.

The maturity in these children is amazing. They already have become models and leaders for others—just in the way they handle their lives. They learned something that some people do not learn in their whole lives. They are angels distributing strength to others; they can offer their inner knowledge in many ways, and only time will tell as to how they chose to express this knowledge and understanding.

LETICIA, 18

No life has a single defining moment in it, and mine is no exception. That would be like saying there was only one person in my life who has had an effect on me, when there are at least ten people each day who make my life a little better than it was before. Yet, throughout the course of my life, there is one person who has disrupted it in the most wonderful manner I can think of. She is my two-year-old sister, Maddison, and she has Down syndrome.

After my mother and stepfather were married during my freshman year of high school, I was still adjusting to the atmosphere of two new men in my life, my stepfather and stepbrother. I had always been an only child and knew very little about the mysteries of having a sibling. So when my mother and stepfather introduced the idea of having a new baby shortly after the marriage had begun, I considered it a distant and unrealistic "threat" to my overwhelmed teenage world. But after my newly espoused parents returned from their honeymoon, they informed my stepbrother and me of my mother's pregnancy. Suddenly it was too late to turn back, the baby was coming.

When she was born, Maddison was premature, though she came rather late in my life. When the doctor told my family that Maddison was born with a disability, none of us could look each other in the eyes for days. When we learned that she had a major heart defect that would have to be corrected by open-heart surgery, this new nightmare struck us dumb. She was confined to stay in the hospital for weeks, fed through a tube in her nose while doctors poked and prodded. More than anything, we wondered why this was happening to her, an innocent baby, and we marveled at the effects of a simple chromosome mutation while we waited for Maddison to come home. We educated ourselves on how to take care of a child in her position, dabbling in sign language to help her communicate and talking with other parents who had children of their own with Down syndrome.

Armed with this knowledge, it took imagination and patience more than anything else to help Maddison adjust to the world she couldn't wait to enter. The reason I say "we" is because, while my parents are her own first and foremost, my stepbrother and I inevitably became her guardians whenever they could not. At first, this responsibility seemed to put a stake right through the "normalcy" of my life. Maddison has never been an easy child. She is fussy and sometimes hard to please, not to mention too mischievous for her own good. Yet now I find these faults endearing. I have fun doing things that are so simple, like reading her stories, giving her a bath, or pacifying her with song when the occasion calls for it, and it often does. And although I'm sure my friends often tire of my constant stories about the hilarious new thing that she has learned to do or the new word she said, they all adore her. I can't think of many people who haven't experienced love at first sight upon seeing Maddison's shining face.

Throughout my teenage years, the idea that spiraled around in my mind was that I must make a mark in the world and do something immensely important to be remembered and be considered worthy of respect. I spent quite a long part of my life questioning my own abilities and who I wanted to become. My fears about whether I had enough talent to pursue a career as a writer sometimes kept me from expressing myself in the way that I wanted to. Yet, when I see how Maddison touches the lives of everyone she comes into contact with, I wonder if she holds all the secrets of the universe in her babbling baby speech. Although she is only two, there are no doubts in her innocent mind and no hindrances either. The person who she is, imperfections and all, is nothing short of a gift, and anyone who would know her as well as I do would feel blessed to have known her at all. Maddison's effect on me is one of inspiration, whether it is for my writing or for my happiness, and I know that if I truly wish to fulfill my dreams, I must cut my proverbial strings and let myself go.

Not everyone in the world is as understanding about how different Maddison is as my friends, and I won't always be there to protect her. The result of her life is in no one's hands but her own, and I worry about what that result will be. Still, I am confident that Maddison will continue to teach me something every day, even if it is a reminder of the same lesson. No matter what is happening in my life, to see her brilliant smile is to see love in its truest form, and that never fails to heal me. Now I can truly understand that no matter what kind of person you are, you can contribute to the world in a number of extraordinary ways, whether you cure a disease or help a child learn to read. Sometimes the simplest things in life are the ones to be treasured.

ARMANDE, 10

My name is Armando Ort and my brother is Francis Christiano. I went through SEVEN years of my brother not knowing if he is going to live or not. I went through seven years of praying, crying and staying right by his side. Hoping that he would make it. But one day it stuck him with force. But my prayers came though and God gave him the strength to get through it.

But we put our guard down too early and a tumor bursted from my brother's head. But I never stopped praying and pouring my strength and blood into them. Then he got through it and now he is almost finished with his treatment. But this time we will never put our guard down. No matter what he goes through I will be by his side know matter how fatal. I will be with him forever.

CATHERINE, 17, NEW CANAAN, CONNECTICUT

It was a cool day, October 26, 1987 to be exact. I was at home with my Aunt Lesley, who is my mother's older sister. My parents were at Bridgeport Hospital. My mom was about to have another baby. My aunt and I were patiently awaiting the phone call that would tell me I had a new sibling and to come to the hospital to see the new baby. It seemed like forever for the call to come in. When it finally came in my aunt did not look as happy as I would have expected. I was three at the time and although this story has been regenerated many times, I have heard my parents tell it, I remember it like it was yesterday.

My aunt got the call that I had a new baby brother; James Vincent Beard would be his name. My dad told my aunt that my mother was fine but that there was something wrong with James and they were not sure what it was. My aunt took me down to the hospital to see my parents and my new baby brother. Until I got to the hospital I did not really know exactly what was going on.

After we talked to my mom and dad for a few minutes, they explained to my aunt and me what was wrong with James. When James was born he was very sick. The doctors had not seen anyone like him before so they did not know what was wrong with him. The photo memory that sticks in my mind the most during his long stay in the hospital was the way he looked. He was so tiny and his little feet and hands, and his tiny, tiny head. He looked like a doll. They couldn't find anything small enough to fit him, so he had to wear doll cloths for the longest time. He was in a very special bed called an incubator because they were not sure what was wrong with him, and they didn't want to take any chances of him spreading something or catching something. He had a feeding tube in his nose because he couldn't swallow anything. I don't remember exactly how long he was in the hospital because he was so little but I do remember when he came home. Things changed. My mom couldn't work. My brother was still so small. At the time the "in" toys for girls were dolls and we were making these throwaway diapers for our dolls. Those were the diapers my brother had to wear. That is how tiny he was. He still had to be fed through a feeding tube. They told us that my brother would probably never live to see his third birthday.

On October 26, 1990 James acted as a normal one-year-old baby would. He would crawl and scoot around on the floor on his hands and knees. He couldn't walk. He still couldn't talk and the doctors said that he wouldn't make it past ten. The doctors also told us that if he did make it past ten he would be nothing but a vegetable all of his life. He would not be able to walk or talk.

The doctors underestimated James greatly. I think was about 5 or 6. It was right around Thanksgiving. My mother, father, James and I were sitting in the living room watching TV. James had crawled over to the coffee table and had stood up holding on to it like he always did. He would try to walk around the table holding on to it for balance. We were not really paying attention to him because he always did this. My dad at that point looked up, and my brother was looking at him. James then let go of the table and walked access the room, about 8 or 10 feet, to my father. We were all in utter shock. James, the one the doctors said would be a vegetable, just got up and walked across the room with no assistance from anyone.

James would continue to grow and impress us more and more each day. Today James is thirteen, soon to be fourteen. He got the walking thing down; we can't even keep up with him anymore. He still can not talk to us verbally, but they have been teaching him sign language at school. For him, he has a large vocabulary. He is learning new words all of the time. They still don't have a specific disorder for him other than the fact that he is both physically and mentally handicapped. He is still small for his age and he has to have growth hormones. Other than the more obvious things that are wrong with him, he is a healthy "normal" teenager.

I think by having a brother like James and by having to go through some of the things my family and I went through, I have been changed in many ways. Some are clear and some are not. I think one of the more noticeable ones is that, without thinking, I would never let anyone say anything about my brother. I don't care what is wrong with him or who the person is that said something, I would not let them say anything. He may not have been the same as everyone else but I still love him the same no matter what. I also believe that if James were not my brother and I didn't have to live with someone like him day in and day out, I would not be the person I am today.

I am a junior in high school now and I have been thinking about college and what I want to do a lot. I have decided that I want to be a special education teacher for handicapped children with mental and physical retardation. I know and believe that if I didn't have a brother like James and didn't know how to be with children like him, I would not be looking to go into the profession that I am. James has changed me in many ways. Even though I am the older sister, I look up my brother. To know that he made it through all those hard times and proved all those doctors to be wrong reassures me. I know that I can always do the same in other aspects of life. I don't think I would ever ask for a different life. I would not want a "normal" brother. I think James has changed my whole family and us whether we realize it or not in many different ways. To me, my life is one that is better than anyone else is because it has changed me as a person and I am thankful for that.

CHAD, 11, DUNSFORD, ONTARIO, CANADA
My Little Friend

What is 114 centimeters tall, has a tube in his stomach to be fed through, and never goes anywhere without his Teletubby friend, Po? Give up? It's my little brother, Shane.

Honorable judges and fellow students, I would like to tell you about my brother Shane. Shane was born two weeks early and that was the last time that he was early at anything.

He did not start to walk until he was three years old and even then he had to hold on to something or someone for support. He was six and a half before he started eating food by mouth. He also has difficulty speaking and because of this he communicates through sign language.

You see, Shane was born with a very rare syndrome called Costello syndrome. This syndrome affects Shane in many ways. The biggest problem is he has difficulty eating, but his size, speech and his ability to run or catch a ball has also been affected.

However, because of the help that Shane has been given by his teachers and the incentive his classmates have given him, he has overcome many of his challenges. Shane's teachers have taught him how to communicate through sign language and the use of a computer in his classroom. The kids in his class have learned from Shane that even if he may look a little different on the outside, he is just like them on the inside. Shane seems to have a magical smile that makes people of all ages want to get to know him better. Because of this, his classmates have become very close to him. They are always eager to help out if he has a problem doing something. When it is time for lunch they understand that Shane does not eat the same way they do and have never made fun of him or said that it was gross that he has his lunch fed to him through a tube in his stomach. He is invited to birthday parties and is often asked during summer vacation to come over to their homes for the afternoon.

Shane's peers are not the only ones who have learned from him. I have also learned a lot from Shane. I have learned about his syndrome, I have learned to accept people for who they really are and not how they look. Most of all, Shane has taught me patience.

At home Shane is like any other little brother. He likes playing outside in the summer. Sometimes he needs a little help from me. We have a red power jeep and I have to make sure that he doesn't fall out when we are going downhill. He also loves our swing set and slide. When we play inside he likes to play games like Sorry. And he loves to watch movies with me.

So if you happen to see a little boy with blond curly hair walking around with a little red Teletubby named Po, stop and say, "Hi Shane," and when he gives you that big magical smile you will understand why he is not just my little brother but he is also my best friend.

DAVID, 16, NEW HAVEN, CONNECTICUT

My favorite and vivid memory of my brother, Jacob, is when we went to Disney World last year. We were at the Magic Kingdom and our family decided to go on Splash Mountain together. Jacob, my seven-year-old brother with Down syndrome, had no idea what to expect of the seven-story water coaster. As our "log" was slowly progressing up the mammoth of a future plunge, he started to have a desperate anxiety attack to get off the ride. While Brer Rabbit and his robotic animal friends were singing their little happy song, the only song Jacob was singing was, "I wanna get off!" His desperation cry was too late as our roller coaster car plummeted down seven stories of roaring water. As our family got off the ride, soaked to every inch of our bodies, Jacob was overjoyed with the fact that he had just plunged into the depths of Space Mountain.

We asked if he wanted to go on the ride again, and while showing the same expression of anxiety and fright as he did on the ride, he quickly replied, "YES!" as he bounded off in the direction of the coasters. Going on Splash Mountain not once, not twice, but three times, Jacob was the happiest kid on the planet. And while walking off with him on my shoulders, I was the happiest brother in the world.

———

The stories sent to us express the joy of acceptance in having a sibling who is struggling with an illness. They reveal an inner peace that many individuals never realize. These children have a message that the world can hear and learn: The journey and acceptance—along with faith—bring a sense of joy and peace. Their simplicity has allowed them to gain strength and they tell us what they know with their innocence. These stories are here to teach us all that there is inspiration derived from turning a hard life into one of true happiness.

Chapter 10

START TO HELP YOUR CHILD RIGHT NOW

❦

*"The road has seemed like a "detour route,"
but it's really just an "alternate plan."*

*"We should encourage our children to talk to us
about their real feelings without the fear of judgment."*

PARENTS WANT TO do what is best for all of their children, but raising a child who is sick or physically or mentally challenged is not something we expected. We are not perfect, yet we want to be the best parents possible for all of our children, as we learn how to balance everything in our busy lives. Please remember that the path of your family has been walked by many a journeyman and you are in wonderful company. Every one of us is learning and growing though our challenges and we are better people for it.

Spiritual leaders in all religions encourage meditation and prayer and likewise we, in our complex lives, will gain confidence in our actions and warmth within our hearts when we pray and meditate. We will know that we are doing the right thing each day. It is a pattern we should start to incorporate into our every day, and also teach our children this important "spiritual quotient."

Next, we should encourage our children to talk to us about their real feelings without the fear of judgment. Once children understand that they are in a safe place of conversation, they will be able to open up to you and others, bringing an open mind. It is important to think of all of the people who can be of assistance to you and your children. You need to reach out to them so that they can step forward to be your support soldiers in times of need. Teachers and other care-givers have seen children struggling before. They want to help, yet sometimes you may need to guide them in the con-versation. Most of the time they have not been where you are, and not all teachers are proficient in this special skill. They can still offer assistance emotionally and often give guidance and structure in school throughout the day.

Remember that the children should be allowed to be an-gry, but also be encouraged to explain their anger. Like an onion that peals its layers to reveal a new skin, so will your child show new strength and energy when they are encour-aged to follow positive steps. We don't always realize the power within us to find strength and compassion in times of stress. Sometimes it is in going through stress—and learning how to handle the stress—that helps us grow spiritually the most. One of our past presidents, Richard Nixon, who un-derwent an enormous pressure because of his bad decisions while president, said, "It is only when you have been in the darkness of the valley that you know how beautiful it is to be on the mountaintop." Like all of us who have struggled with our own challenges, although not necessarily through bad choices, we know how wonderful that mountaintop can be. This appreciation comes when we learn to accept our more difficult situations and find peace in the embracing of our life.

We see in these stories the ability to see the goodness in life, to find happiness in the little things, and appreciate every day. Actually, these children find the joy of life much more abundantly than most children.

The views from within the families of a sick child are very different from the rest of society. There are too many children in this country who are waiting to receive the next present or trip they think they deserve. They have not seen the complexities of life and they have not had the character-building experiences that having a sick brother and sister can bring. They do not comprehend what these siblings deal with every day. Often when we are not forced to be more than we naturally are, we can become self-absorbed and sometimes narcissistic.

Your child is special. They seek a happy life and need to know that they are loved. We need to assure them with love, time and discussion to enable their metamorphosis into caring, patient sisters and brothers. They can open the doors to see the possibilities for themselves through the exercises.

Painting, writing and singing are wonderful ways to enable them to blossom. Week by week they will open to the joy that is in their life and they will embrace the goodness of the family they have.

Chapter 11

GROW AS A FAMILY

∝∾

*"Like an onion that peals its layers to reveal a new
skin, so will your child show new strength and energy
when they are encouraged to follow positive steps."*

IN A WORLD of challenges we have a responsibility to
guide each other and look to God for faith and inspiration.
As I learned, we need someone to tell us how to pull the parachute cord as we leave the plane so that we can glide towards
the earth and land without too many bruises. The children's
stories help us find that cord so our landing is safe. We can
be assured that we will understand each other's differences
on the journey to peace and acceptance of life.

No one promised that the sun would shine every day, but
we hope it does most days. There were no guarantees that
we would be worth a million dollars just because we worked
hard, but we can always hope that it might come our way. We
all wish for perfect health but most of us will suffer some illness in our lives. Difficult things cannot stand in the way of
happiness.

The children who have a sister or brother who is ill know
most of these things at a very young age. They are more in
tune with the realities of life that are presented to us at any
time. Their messages are clear indicators of the responsibilities that we sometimes do not want to see and hear. I consider them our angels who are sending monumental messages
of life's real lessons. They instruct us as to what is significant

in all of our lives.

By sharing the lessons of the children we hope to open up a dialogue that is instrumental in helping many people who are struggling with life. We hope to help people who are angry that things are not perfect, and address those who are disappointed they can't have a life without challenges.

If you have someone in your family who is sick in any way, please reach out to let them know how you feel. It is important to try to understand their differences and challenges.

Power is in the gentleness and goodness of each individual, not in the domination of any person or the accumulation of wealth. It is in the gentle touch, the kind word or a soft smile that is medicinal in making us whole and strong.

Power is in the lifting of others' spirits and in the feeding of their souls, not in the awards or adorations. It is in the time offered, the listening and the caring, that we all will come to understand the significance of the children's stories. For it is in *Day by Day* that we grow.

Constructive Thoughts
to Guide Families

1. How can we help with the confusion that the sister and brother are coping with? While it can be difficult to take time when we are overwhelmed, the entire family is going through a huge transition and a unique learning experience. You may want to write down what has happened that has changed your family and discuss it together.

2. Children may not want to talk about their feelings because they are confused about their guilt and anger. It is healthy to help them express these filling in their own words and their own time frame.

3. When you prepare questions to open productive discussion it will be easier for you both. This is very beneficial for the stage of the growth process. This enables you to think about what both of you may need to explore with your talks.

4. Bring yourself back to your childhood and remember when you were scared and angry. This will help you understand the emotions of the children. Explain that you know that they have a right to be angry. Their lives have been turned upside down.

5. Together parents and children can make lists of activities they could do together so that the siblings feel the love that they may feel has diminished because of what is happening around them.

6. Encourage children to write journals, both as a remembrance of their growth and as a catharsis for their experiences. They can write about how they feel they are different, why they are special and how they can tell others about their feelings. This will be a support through the transitional stages.

7. Reach out to professionals and explain what your family is encountering in everyday life. Teachers, caregivers, ministers, priests, rabbis and friends will not understand the complexity of the situation without your guidance.

General Sibling Support Groups for All Illnesses

DONALD MEYER'S SIBLING SUPPORT PROJECT
www.siblingsupport.org
Organization dedicated to the life long concerns of
brothers and sisters of children with special health,
developmental and mental health concerns.

DAILY STRENGTH
www.dailystrength.org/support

FAMILY VOICES
www.familyvoices.org

KIDS HEALTH
www.kidshealth.org
Provided by the Nemours Foundation, KidsHealth
provides families with accurate, up-to-date, and
jargon-free health information they can use.

KIDSAID.COM
Support for children of all ages and all illnesses.

KIDS TOGETHER
www.kidstogether.org
National support for families with disabilities.

MOTHERS FROM HELL
    www.mothersfromhell2.org
    Support and advocacy for families of children with any
    type of disability.

Support Groups by Illness or Disability

AIDS/HIV
    www.cellscience.com/hivcharities
    Cell Science is a national directory of support groups.

ARTHRITIS
    www.arthritis.org/chaptermap.php
    www.arthritissupport.com/supportgroups

ASTHMA LUNGS AND RESPIRATION
    www.aafa.org
    Asthma and Allergy Foundation of America's "Find a
    Support Group."

AUTISM
    www.nationalautismassociation.org/localchapter.php
    Local Chapters of the National Autism Association.

    www.jbtautism.org/nsupport.html
    Jacob's Bridge Through Autism lists national support
    groups.

BIRTH DISORDERS
    www.marchofdimes.com
    www.birthdefects.org

BRAIN TUMOR

www.cbtf.org

Children's Brain Tumor Foundation

www.abta.org

American Brain Tumor Foundation's "Reaching Out for Support" guide.

www.abta.org/kids/sharing/index.htm

Online message boards for kids from the American Brain Tumor Foundation.

CANCER

www.cancercare.org/get_help/special_progs/cc_for_kids.php

Cancer Care offer support for families who have someone who is ill.

www.acor.org

Association for Cancer Online Resources

www.acor.org/ped-onc/cfissues/camps.html

www.campparents.org

Camps for Kids

www.candlelighters.org/Affiliates.stm

Candlelighers is a support group for children with cancer.

www.gildasclub.org

Gilda's Club offers support for the entire family when someone has cancer.

www.leukemia-lymphoma.org
Nationwide listing of support groups for blood related
illnesses.

www.supersibs.org
Support for siblings of children with cancer.

CARDIOVASCULAR DISEASE
www.americanheart.org
www.mendedhearts.org
Cerebral Palsy or Cystic Fibrosis

CEREBRAL PALSY
www.hemi-kids.org
Hemi Kids

www.ucp.org/ucp_channelsub.cfm
State by state resource guide from United Cerbral Palsy.

CROHN'S & COLITIS
www.ccfa.org

COSTELLO SYNDROME
http://body.aol.com/conditions/costello-syndrome
United States Costello Syndrome Family Network

www.costellokids.org.uk/
Costello Kids is an international support group based in
the UK.

CYSTIC FIBROSIS
   www.cff.org/aboutCFFoundation/Locations/
   FindAChapter/
   National and local listings for Cystic Fibrosis support.

   www.cellscience.com/CFCharities

DIABETES
   www.defeatdiabetes.org
   www.juvenilediabetesfoundation.org
   www.childrenwithdiabetes.com/support

DOWN SYNDROME
   www.ndss.org
   National Down Syndrome Society's listing of affiliates/
   support groups.

EPILEPSY
   www.epilepsyfoundation.org

EYE DISORDERS
   www.preventblindness.org/cgi-bin/htsearch

KIDNEY DISEASE
   www.kidney.org
   National Kidney Foundation

GENETIC
   www.rarediseases.org/programs/networking

HEMOPHILIA
   www.hemophilia.org

FIBRODYSPLASIA OSSIFICANS PROGRESSIVA
www.ifopa.org

LEUKODYSTROPHY
www.ulf.org

PRIMARY IMMUNODEFICIENCY DISEASE
www.infopi.org

SICKLE CELL ANEMIA
www.sicklecellkids.org/
www.sicklecelldisease.org/resources

RHETT-SYNDROME
http://dailystrength.org/support-groups/Developmental_
Learning_Disorders/Rett_Syndrome
Online support from Daily Strength.

TAY-SACHS
www.ntsad.org

WISKOTT-ALDRICH SYNDROME
www.mdjunction.com
www.rarediseases.about.com

MENTAL DISABILITY
www.nmha.org/go/searchMHA
Mental Health of America Affiliate Directory

www.nami.org
National Alliance on Mental Illness State and Local
Guide.

Neurological Disorders

STROKES
  www.KidsHaveStrokes.org

  www.hemikids.org
  Hemi-Kids (also for Cerebral Palsy)

HYDROCEPHALUS
  www.nhfonline.org/aboutus.php
  www.hydroassoc.org

NARCOLEPSY
  www.narcolepsynetwork.org/link.php

OBESITY
  www.obesityinamerica.org
  Obesity in America Organization List of Support
  Groups.

MENTAL DISABILITY
  www.nmha.org/go/searchMHA
  Mental Health of America Affiliate Directory

  www.nami.org
  National Alliance on Mental Illness State and Local
  Guide.

  www.bestbuddies.org
  Best Buddies enhances the lives of people with intellectual disabilities.

SPINA BIFIDA
www.spinabifidaassociation.org
Resources and links for Spina Bifida Associations.

Stories by Illness

Mallory: autism
Katie: spinal bifida
Justin: brain tumor—atypical teratoid rhabdoid tumor

CHAPTER 7
Lauren: immunodeficiency
Nicole: autism
Karen: autism
Emily: cancer—leukemia
Tyro: meningitis, hydrocephalus, epilepsy
Emily: mental illness

CHAPTER 8
Courtenay: Rhett syndrome
Stephanie: cancer—leukemia
Farryl: Down syndrome
Emily: brain tumor—left temporal lobe astrocytoma

CHAPTER 9
Leticia: Down syndrome
Armando: brain tumor
Catherine: mental disability, physical disability
Chad: Costello syndrome
David: Down syndrome

Acknowledgments

THERE ARE SO many individuals that I would like to acknowledge. I was blessed with the editing skills of Lese Dunton and with the book organization and layout from Juli Huss. Their inspiration and spirituality brought a positive hope to everything we did. Jim Guiher added thoughtful ideas and concepts to our book. Thank you Jim. To Dr. Diana Beardsley, Dr. Richard Edelson, Anita Nirenberg, MS, RN and Sheila Santacroce, PhD, APMN. They understood our mission and helped us to get this book to the place where it is. Special gratitude to my friends at Yale-New Haven Hospital and Yale Medical School, especially Connie Nicolosi, Pediatric Oncology Social Worker and Erin Spaulding, Child Life Specialist, who helped to gather our stories and also to Hackensack Medical Center's Judy Solomon, LCSW, MPH, Supervisor of Tomorrows Children, and Ellen Goldring, Chief of Child Life and Creative Arts Therapy, who gathered stories and completely understood our mission. To Tracy Moore and Joe Jay from the Children's Brian Tumor Foundation. whose support was outstanding. To First Lady Barbara Bush, who has been a source of great strength and guidance since we met in 2003.

To the corporations and foundations who lent support including Barclays Capital, The William E. Simon Foundation, Bonaventura Devine Foundation, Wendy Schmidt, Futures and Options for Kids, the Board of Trustees of the Richard D. Frisbee III Foundation and so many others, who, along the years, brought the Foundation to where we are today.

Finally, I would like to thank all the sisters and brothers who contributed their inspiring stories. They opened their hearts while teaching us valuable lessons.

About the Author

CHRISTINE FRISBEE, the third of twelve children, has always been interested in sibling relationships. She and her husband, Rick, have five children. After their second child died of leukemia in 1989, she worked at the Yale School of Medicine with families who were looking for an unrelated donor for a bone marrow transplant. Her experience and work inspired her to write this book. She has interviewed children and professionals in many organizations about the impact that childhood illness has within the family. Christine attended Columbia School of Social Work and has an MBA from the University of Connecticut. She has been chairman of the Richard D. Frisbee III Foundation since it was founded in 1990. Christine and her husband Rick live in New York City.

Richard D. Frisbee III
Foundation

www.frisbeefoundation.org

THE PROCEEDS FROM this book will go to support the Frisbee Foundation. The mission of the Foundation is to support basic and clinical research to further understanding and treatment for childhood and adult cancers and related bone marrow diseases; advance the application of bone marrow and stem cell transplantation for treatment; establish support systems for patients and their families during treatment and provide ongoing educational programs for health care professionals. The Foundation grew over the years and we have funded programs that reach beyond our initial mission to include support for siblings of children will all illnesses and their families.

Printed in the United States
114780LV00001B/16-111/P